The
Parents' Pipeline Guide

Plain Talk About Teens and Alcohol, Drugs, Sex,
Eating Disorders and Depression

Written by
Sheila Fuller & Leigh Rudd

Edited by
Robert F. Fuller

Illustrated by
Andrew Nolan Mensing

Published by Parents' Pipeline, Inc.
Greenwich, Connecticut 06831
1995

Cover photo: Bob Capazzo
Authors' photos: Alayne Burger
Art direction: James Miller

Children are our most precious resource.
Preparing them for the future should be our first priority.

To Our Children

Allison and Andy
Amanda, Jason and Michael

Acknowledgments

The authors gratefully acknowledge the invaluable advice and support of the following individuals and organizations.

Nancy Bronson, Ph.D; Paul S. Builter; Raymond D. Builter; Guy Cabral, Ph.D; Sue Carlson, Program Director and Laura Young, Education Coordinator, Alcohol and Drug Abuse Council; Ann Caron, Ed.D., author; Henry Crawford, Youth Supervisor, Stamford Police; Sue Denis, Nurse and Health Educator; Robert Gilkeson, M.D.; Jacquie Gordon, author; Barry Halpin, M.A., Prevention Specialist, Youth Options; Angela Kaufman, Alcohol Counselor, Stamford Hospital; Karin Kyles, Executive Director, CT Communities for Drug-Free Youth, Inc.; Ed Krumeich and Philip Russell, attorneys; Chad McDonald, substance abuse counselor; Elizabeth McKay, C.S.W., A.C.S.W.; Diane Mickley, M.D., Director of the Wilkins Center for Eating Disorders and President of The American Anorexia and Bulimia Association; Otto and Connie Moulton, Committees of Correspondence; Christopher Nolan; Mary-K. O'Sullivan, M.A., CRPS, NCADC, Trainer, The Center: Learning Resource for Substance Abuse and Health; Cheryl Pickering, Alcohol and Drug Abuse Counselor, Meridien Council; Ann Sadowsky, Executive Director of Lower Fairfield Co. AACD; Jeffrey Burke Satinover, M.D.; Jonathan Schwenke; Jason Simpson, paralegal; Veronica Skerker, Health Ed. Consultant, CT Dept. of Ed.; Liz and Bill Taggart; Forest Tennant, M.D., Community Health Project Medical Group; Barbara Wyatt, The Parents' Music Resource Center; the Fairfield Police; The Greenwich Council on Youth and Drugs, Inc.; the Greenwich Police Department; PRIDE; Parents Together. With special thanks to Patty Brooks Walker for her support and contributions to this guide.

COPYRIGHT NOTICE

Cautions

The various programs, activities, facilities, services and the like referred to in this guide are believed to be representative of those available to concerned parents, but our listings do not purport to be comprehensive. To suggest another program, activity, facility or service for inclusion in future editions, please write Parents' Pipeline, Inc., P.O. Box 11037, Greenwich, CT 06831-1037. Our inclusion herein of a program, activity, facility or service does not constitute an endorsement on our part nor a representation by us as to quality of service or efficiency of response or care.

Opinions offered in this guide are nonprofessional and are offered in the field of parenting only. Although based on interviews with professionals and others claiming expertise, the information herein provided is not intended to be used and should not be used as a substitute for timely professional counseling and treatment in respect of drug-related, alcohol-related, emotional or behavioral problems of the young.

The authors have taken care to confirm the accuracy of factual information contained in this guide, but can assume no liability or responsibility for errors or omissions in respect of such information. Organizations and the scope of their services change, as do addresses and telephone numbers. Readers are invited to draw our attention to factual errors so that corrections can be made in future editions. Furthermore, readers are cautioned to evaluate services, organizations, sitters, activities, etc. as they hire help or join groups at their own risk.

The Twelve Steps which appear on pages 141 and 142 are reprinted with permission of Alcoholics Anonymous World Services, Inc. Permission to reprint the Twelve Steps does not mean that A.A. has reviewed or approved the contents of this publication, nor that A.A. agrees with the views expressed herein. A.A. is a program of recovery from alcoholism — use of the Twelve Steps in connection with programs and activities which are patterned after A.A., but which address other problems, does not imply otherwise.

Introduction

Parents of adolescents everywhere can quickly identify with this Guide's cover photo. In today's world, however, messy rooms are the least of the problems we face trying to raise teenagers.

American culture has changed radically over the past 30 years. New entries in the vocabulary such as burnout, bad trip, O.D.'ing, bingeing and purging, date rape, safe sex and latchkey kids give testimony to the change. Statistics suggest that the deterioration of our society is far more than a figment of our imaginations.

Consider former drug 'czar' William Bennett's 'cultural indicators' which compare the early 60's with the early 90's. Since 1963:

- Crime (most of it alcohol or drug related) among teens has risen 560%.
- Teen suicide, usually alcohol or drug related, has tripled.
- Illegitimate births to teens have increased 400%.
- Divorce rates have quadrupled and the number of children living in single parent homes has tripled.
- SAT scores have dropped, on average, 80 points.

If you are not convinced of the extent to which things have changed, you may want to do some unscientific research of your own. Ask people you know who are in their late forties or older how many of their friends died in alcohol or drug related accidents or by suicide or homicide when they were growing up. Ask how many classmates had to leave middle school or high school to enter an institution to recover from an addiction or overcome anorexia or bulimia. How many had to 'do time'?

Very likely, they will answer 'no one'; say that their schools were drug-free; and they will tell you that they never heard of eating disorders until they were thirty-five. On the subject of abortion or illegitimate births, they'll probably say that people who made babies got married. Chances are none of their classmates were arrested for carrying concealed weapons.

Ask any city or suburban 18 year-old the same questions and he or she will name car accident victims, suicide victims, kids who've been arrested for toting weapons or pushing drugs, friends who have joined

AA, girls who have had abortions or left school to have illegitimate babies and classmates who have been institutionalized.

Times Have Changed, Not Kids

Does this mean that adolescents today are somehow different than they used to be? Not really. From time immemorial, young people in the process of breaking away have gone out and done exactly what adults have told them not to. Tom Sawyer is a good example, or Romeo and Juliet, not to mention the Prodigal Son. Psychologist Lee Salk once said that if your children haven't gotten into some kind of trouble by the age of 16, you're not raising them right.

If not teenagers themselves, what <u>has</u> changed? Why is there so much more opportunity for kids to engage in negative and even life-threatening behavior? Why do many young people today appear to have no concept of the danger or immorality of what they're doing?

Depending on which expert you ask, the explanation lies in either modern parenting, the breakdown of the criminal justice system, the decline of education, religious dissipation, the media, rock music, availability of drugs, affluence, or poverty. No doubt all of these social influences have contributed in one way or another.

Parents Are #1

Whatever the contributing factors may be, there is one thing the experts agree on — and that is that parents are still the #1 influence on their children. Therein lies the hope — and the reason for The Parents' Pipeline Guide. After reading this Guide, parents will have a clear picture of the dark side of the adolescent world and they will have a better idea of how to deal with it. With this knowledge, they can use their influence to protect their children and diminish the pressures that seduce them into self-destructive behavior.

What's In the Guide

The Parents' Pipeline Guide is divided into three sections:

The *Prevention* section describes approaches parents and communities have applied to head off trouble before it starts, both within the family and within the neighborhood, town or city.

The *Problems* section gives specific facts about teenage alcohol and other drug abuse, sexual activity, eating disorders, depression and crime to help parents recognize clues that can alert them to the possibility that their child might be in trouble. This section also includes (1) reasons why teens indulge in destructive behavior and (2) a discussion of rock and media influences.

The *Help For Parents* section discusses in detail the recovery process including steps parents need to take to get treatment for a troubled teen. This section also provides an overview of legal obligations and lists state and national contacts which offer help to parents who don't know where to turn.

The Guide is tabbed to help you find subjects of particular interest easily. But the authors hope that in time you will read the entire book. Taken as a whole, it paints a picture of an adolescent world which desperately needs changing. Even the best-behaved children come out of adolescence shell-shocked because of what they've watched happen to their friends and classmates. At a time when they need more support from their parents, kids are getting less. Changing their world should be the first priority of every one of us who has children. Nothing less than the future of our country depends on it.

Table of Contents

Prevention

Problems

Help for Parents

Prevention

Communicate with your children.
Nothing is solved in silence.

Vital Steps to Clear Communication

Make yourself available — Round the clock. Children do not confide in parents who seem to be too absorbed in other matters to care.

Never reject your child — reject only the bad behavior. Don't give up on your child, no matter what he or she has done.

Talk — If you or your child suffers in silence, nothing will get solved. It is especially important to talk when things are at their worst.

Be open — Don't assume your child knows what you expect of him/her. Make it clear.

Listen — Really hear what your child is saying and don't interrupt.

Stay calm — People cannot communicate through fits of anger.

Avoid sarcasm — Derision closes conversation.

Stick to the issue — Don't nag about past transgressions or predict future ones.

Be consistent — By punishing wrong behavior on one occasion and ignoring it the next, we confuse our children.

Stand firm — Don't get pushed off a stand you've taken on drinking, partying or curfew, or soon your children will ignore your rules.

Trust — Your child needs to feel that you trust him/her to make good decisions. If your child breaks your trust, you need to re-establish it.

3

**It's not always easy for working mothers
and fathers to balance work and family.**

Effective Parenting

Find Time

If you don't find time for your kids... the alcohol, drug and sex peddlers will!

Turning away from work and other distractions and focusing on our children is a surprisingly difficult yet essential duty of parenting. Make your children your top priority. A common complaint from today's teens is "My parents give me their money, but not their time or their attention." There is evidence that teenagers who believe that their parents 'really care' get through the worst of situations and emerge from adolescence whole and happy. We show our children that we care by being available *even when we are at work,* by focusing on what's important to them when we are with them, by re-establishing trust when they have broken it and by setting rules and guidelines which hold them to a high standard.

Set an Example
If parents are the #1 influence on their children, and studies indicate that they are, then it seems axiomatic that we cannot expect our children to behave better than we ourselves do. By curbing our drinking or smoking habits and condemning any drug use, watching our language, and restraining our tempers, we can send a strong message to our children. Share with your children an instance where you may have compromised popularity or a business opportunity in order to do what you felt was right. Host intergenerational activities where no one drinks. Young people say their friends won't come to a party unless you serve alcohol. It's not so. They will come. We need to show our kids how to have fun without drinking.

Take Stands and Set Limits

We should not be afraid to establish rules or stick to them. Children need to know what will happen to them if they break the rules. Following through with the consequences is imperative or children will stop taking rules seriously. More than a few troubled teens have been heard to say "Adults don't care about us. They'll let us do anything we want no matter how bad it is for us." When you take a stand, brace yourself. Your teenagers will try to push you off it and they have more energy! Even so, they want your guidance.

Talk Openly

Talk about the negative effects of alcohol, tobacco and other drug abuse.* Excessive drinking makes you throw up and lose control at the very least. It can also kill you. Drug use is a one-way street leading to increasingly painful 'lows' following brief 'highs.' Tobacco is a health hazard. Make it clear that getting caught by parents ought to be a powerful deterrent as well.

Discuss the Reality of Drug Use

Many children are very much 'in the dark' about drugs and don't understand the risks and pitfalls of substance abuse. A 1991 survey done by the Office of the Inspector General reveals that one-third of all students don't understand the intoxicating effects of alcohol and believe that fresh air and coffee will sober you up. Eighty percent do not know that one ounce of whiskey contains as much alcohol as a 12-ounce can of beer, and one-third do not know that wine coolers contain alcohol. A careful reading of the 'Problems' section of this book, beginning on page 31, will give you the specific information you need to alert your child to the dangers and often irreversible damage caused by substance abuse.

*Note: The terms *substance abuse, chemical abuse* and *drug abuse*, unless otherwise specified, refer to the abuse of alcohol and tobacco as well as the abuse of any illicit or prescription drugs.

Explain that the High Doesn't Last

Getting 'high' on alcohol or other drugs doesn't last and you feel worse when the 'high' wears off. Accomplishment is the greatest 'high' there is, and every goal achieved in the adolescent years becomes a building block for the future. Drug/alcohol use short-circuits the teenager's ability to achieve anything.

Don't Enable

In our enthusiasm to protect our children or to insure their popularity, we sometimes encourage the wrong behavior. If we really want to protect them, we should let them sit out a game when they forget their sneakers rather than rush over with the missing shoes. We should let them serve detention if they oversleep rather than write them an excuse. We should refuse to buy the keg, rather than buy it and pray no harm comes to them. If we save our children for a day by 'preventing their drinking and driving', but set them up for a life of alcoholism by allowing them to drink, we haven't really helped them. We should resist the temptation to protect them from consequences when school officials want to impose punishment or even when police arrest them. A week's suspension or a visit to the county juvenile office can go a long way in preventing a second occurrence of pot possession, vandalism, or drunk driving.

Communicate Values

We need to discuss our views with our children on drinking, drugging, sex, lying, cheating, shirking duties, whatever. A middle class boy arrested for theft was quoted as saying "It's degrading to work in a grocery store at $5.00 an hour, and it's so easy to steal and sell car radios for $100." Some of our high schoolers believe it's O.K. to drink themselves blind as long as they are not the designated driver. Some sons think 'no' means 'yes' when it comes to sex. We can't expect our children to uphold our values if they don't know what they are. Make your views clear to your children. When your child is caught in a moral dilemma, help him or her dissect it and see what is right and wrong about it.

Ask the Right Questions

Parents often open conversation with questions which cut their children off. "Did you get an 'A' in English?" "Did you score a goal?" "Who'd you play with?" If your child got a 'C', failed to score a goal or has been rejected by a popular group, he or she will be driven away by such questions. Talk about a book he or she is reading or something on TV or even the school lunch menu. Eventually your children will get around to talking about what matters.

Limit TV

Unless the whole family is watching something special, turn it off. If you're just watching TV rather than watching something that really matters, you're wasting time. Play a game with your children, read aloud, go rock climbing, build a tree house, play ball, go fishing, construct a model plane, bake a cake, ride the rapids, whatever. Together, find better things to do. That's the fun of having kids. Enjoy them. Before you know it, they'll be gone!

Monitor Rock Music

From 6th grade to 12th, children listen to approximately 11,000 hours of rock music(1). Much of it is harmless and fun. But a good deal of it glorifies such themes as drug use, the occult, bondage and sado-masochism, explicit sex and violence toward women. See page 47 for a detailed discussion of rock and rap.

Be Aware of Media Influence

Cigarette smoking is on the rise with kids. A recent study showed that one cigarette company greatly increased its share of the age 18 and under market after introducing a mascot with youth appeal. The average teen will view 75,000 beer commercials before the age of 18 (2). They will see very few ads urging them not to smoke and drink. See pages 53 to 61 for a detailed discussion of media and advertising.

Please Note: Numbers in parentheses in this *Prevention* section are keyed to the numbered list of statistical reference materials which begins on page i.

Teach Negotiating Skills

Unless a child has to negotiate to use a car, watch a particular program, use the telephone or defer in other ways, he will never learn to share or compromise. Children who do not learn to share or compromise have no humility and no concept of the importance of others. They grow up to be rude drivers, disagreeable co-workers and inconsiderate spouses.

Make Children Accountable

Children who are not made accountable are wasteful at best and can be self-destructive. A sad example is a 16 year-old who reported that by giving him a generous allowance his parents were supporting his drug habit, only they didn't know it. He didn't want them to know, because they might stop the flow of money.

Keep Children Busy

There are many ways to keep young people busy. Some useful suggestions appear in the next section of this book (Parents and Community). Nobody gets into trouble faster than an idle teen. Consider the case of four latchkey teens who took to doing inhalants during the afternoons after school. One day they blew themselves up when one of them lit a cigarette while they were inhaling butane gas. If we cut down the opportunity for trouble, we cut down on the trouble.

Seek Help Even If You Just Suspect You Need It

If you are working hard at being a good parent but you still feel that your child is in trouble, you may have a problem which you cannot solve on your own. DON'T LET PROBLEMS GO UNTREATED. The Recovery chapter of this book, beginning on page 131 leads parents through the process of getting help for a troubled child.

It's hard to raise drug-free kids alone in the nineties.
It takes the concerted effort of parents, police, elected officials, clergy and teachers.

Parents and Community

"We must all hang together, or assuredly we shall hang separately."
— At the Signing of the Declaration of Independence, July 4, 1776

Over the past several decades, lifestyles in communities across America have changed radically. In the past, children grew up in multi-generational families and in communities where teachers, doctors and public officials were often long-time family friends. In today's world the majority of families are fragmented (many single-parent); transient neighbors seldom meet; and people work outside the towns they live in and aren't able to get involved in their own communities. Even the time-honored tradition of the family meal is becoming an anachronism as each family member grabs a meal on the run. Commuting parents arrive home just as their children need to go out to sports activities or club meetings. In a monograph on teenage substance abuse, the Office of Substance Abuse Prevention in Washington, D.C. suggests that the media are replacing the family as the major influence in our children's lives. (1)*

Parents and communities throughout the United States realize that we need to rebuild the traditional network of caring adults around our children. Adults from family, church, school and government, working together, give our children the support they need to grow up whole and happy. In many towns adversity has become the mother of invention as leaders are forced to create programs to help young people. Here are some creative approaches that have worked:

Youth Councils or Task Forces

Many communities have formed youth councils or task forces to spearhead activities which enrich the lives of teens. **These usually draw on:**

1. *Concerned parents* willing to volunteer the time it takes to organize parent awareness programs and coordinate drug-free and alcohol-free activities for young people.

2. *Public and private school principals* who work out a program of substance abuse education in local schools and supervise social activities.

* See *Statistical References*, page i

11

3. *The chief of police and a youth officer* who keep their local youth council abreast of drug activity and unsupervised partying and who work to stem these activities.

4. *Physicians* who advise these councils about the effects of drugs and alcohol on the developing adolescent body, the incidence of sexually-transmitted diseases and the kind of physical and psychological problems related to teen substance abuse.

5. *Psychologists, social workers and representatives* from area adolescent treatment centers who advise on rehabilitation and counseling.

6. *Elected representatives* who are prepared to plan and introduce legislation and to help the council find government grant money for its projects.

Youth council or task force members should meet at least monthly in order to plan projects to promote wholesome activities for young people and to oversee their completion.

Successful Youth Projects

To establish the projects listed below, both parents and teens will need to make a significant time commitment. But that's the fun of it – spending your free time with your children working toward a worthwhile goal and enjoying the satisfaction of reaching that goal. Parents will also need to raise funds to support these projects. See page 20 for ideas.

Teen centers — teens have helped renovate shut-down railroad stations or public buildings as teen centers. Programs include socializing, peer leadership training, community service work and recreational activities.

Outdoor programs — young adults with Explorer Scouting and climbing experience have been hired to take teens camping, canoeing, rock climbing and kayaking.

Nighttime organized sports programs - school gymnasiums have been kept open Friday and Saturday nights until midnight for ballgames. Local policemen act as referees. Where necessary, they walk children home after the games.

Work programs — in one tough neighborhood, police bought an abandoned car wash, hired local youths to work in it and used it to wash all the cars in the police fleet. Crime in the neighborhood dropped significantly, partly because the business kept the kids busy and partly because police cars were constantly driving through the area.

Community outreach — bored teens have been mobilized to work to keep their towns green and clean. Many act as big brothers or sisters to children of people who live in local homeless shelters.

Youth leadership conferences — one to three-day youth leadership conferences are held in schools or local conference centers. Authors and speakers who work with adolescents are brought in to lead assemblies and teach seminars. Youth conferences are designed to motivate teens and to raise their self-esteem. Facilitators lead discussions on peer pressure, ethics and techniques for resisting negative influences. Local libraries, bookstores and social agencies ought to be able to help you find a motivational speaker to lead your conference.

Peer training — high school teens who reject alcohol and drugs are trained to talk to middle school children about the pitfalls of substance abuse and to teach them techniques to resist negative peer pressure.

Newsletters — community-wide newsletters have been published and mailed to parents. They include articles about successful parenting techniques, stress management, teen problems and activities for youths. One of the best examples of such a newsletter is published by Parents Together in Greenwich, Connecticut. For a subscription to this newsletter, send a check for $10 to:

PARENTS TOGETHER SUBSCRIPTIONS
P.O. Box 80 - Greenwich, CT 06830

Essay contests — some towns have sponsored essay contests with cash prizes for students who write the best essays on an anti-drug subject.

Alcohol and drug-free parties — many schools are holding chaperoned alcohol and drug-free prom and graduation parties. The parties include raffles and prizes, dancing, games and band competitions and go as late as students wish them to.

Group parent prevention — increasingly, parents with children in the same class are setting common rules and limits for their children as a group. They are succeeding in cutting down on trouble by setting a common curfew, establishing areas which are off-limits, and taking turns policing playgrounds and chaperoning social activities. All the parents of one high school junior class, for example, refused to rent limousines for the class prom, while another group set a weekend curfew of 12:30 a.m. and stuck to a punishment of two weeks' grounding for any child who broke curfew.

Community Cops — originally a New York City program created to alleviate hostility between residents and patrolling police. Components of the program include police walking beats, not just patrolling in cars; police working the same neighborhoods so they get to know the residents and the business owners; police seeing residents safely through dangerous areas; and parents attending seminars to learn what police do and why they work the way they do.

Big Brothers/Big Sisters of America — provides, through its over 500 agencies nationwide, adult volunteers who serve as mentors and role models for school-age children, primarily those from single-parent families. For more information about the programs or volunteer opportunities, look for the Big Brothers/Big Sisters listing in your phone book, or call (215) 567-7000 for the agency nearest you.

Homework clubs — many community organizations sponsor homework clubs where children who need special help can go after school and work with tutors.

Parenting Programs

Parents enjoy and benefit greatly from workshops designed to help them better communicate with their teens and resolve conflicts. The PTA, Planned Parenthood, the Junior League, the YWCA and the YMCA, as well as local community organizations, often sponsor such workshops. If there are no such programs in your area, there are a number of parent training programs which will send teachers to your town to work with parent groups. Parents who graduate from these programs then teach other parents what they have learned. **A representative sampling of available programs follows:**

1. **Parent Effectiveness Training** **(619) 481-8121**

   531 Stevens Avenue
   Solana Beach, CA 92075

   Trained and authorized instructors teach skills for helping children solve their own problems, for influencing children to change unacceptable behavior, for setting rules that are honored and for resolving conflicts amicably. *8 three-hour sessions.*

2. **Parents' Pipeline** **(203) 352-4704**

   Sheila Fuller and Leigh Rudd
   P. O. Box 11037
   Greenwich, CT 06831

   "Take Back The Reins" - Parent workshops designed to empower parents to take control and prevent adolescent drinking, drugging, promiscuity and depression. *2-hr. sessions.*

3. **Los Ninos Bien Educados** **(818) 980-0903**

   Dr. Kerby T. Alvy
   Center for the Improvement of Child Caring
   11331 Ventura Boulevard, Suite 103
   Studio City, CA 91604

   Bilingual, bicultural instructors foster Hispanic-American identity, healthy development and self-esteem, and teach a variety of child management skills. *12 three-hour training sessions.*

4. Effective Black Parenting

Dr. Kerby T. Alvy, same as above.

Emphasis on African-American identity, healthy development and self-esteem. Instructors teach child management skills and strategies.

14 three-hour training sessions.

5. Parent to Parent   (404) 565-5257

Connie Davis
1240 Johnson Ferry Place, Suite F-10
Marietta, GA 30068

Designed to help parents steer their teens away from alcohol and drug abuse.

Three workshops presented in 8 individual segments.

6. National Indian Child Welfare Association   (503) 222-4044

3611 S.W. Hood Street, Suite 201
Portland, OR 97207
Fax. (503) 222-4007

Positive Indian Parenting: Honoring Our Children by Honoring Our Traditions. Culturally specific training for Indian parents.

8 sessions. (They prefer that you write for information.)

Note: when you contact a parent training program, ask the contact person what the program's fee is and ask for an appraisal evaluation of the program to make sure it serves your community's needs.

A more complete list of parent training programs appears in a book called *Parent Training Is Prevention* published by the Office for Substance Abuse Prevention. To obtain a copy, call the National Clearinghouse for Alcohol and Drug Information at (800) 729-6686.

Activities for Young People

The organizations listed below are long-established and have a proven track record of providing wholesome, enriching activities for young people. The advantage of enrolling your child in their activities is that they are low-cost and easy to establish if you don't already have them in your community. All of these organizations have innovative programs which take into account the problems of modern adolescents. **If you write or call the contact listed, someone will help you get any one of these organizations started in your town if you don't have it already.**

Boy Scouts

All Boy Scout programs are administered locally by area Councils. The Council for your region is listed in your area telephone book.

Scouting for adolescents includes Boy Scouting for boys aged 11 through 17 with an emphasis on peer leadership and a vigorous outdoor program. Varsity Scouting for ages 14 through 17 emphasizes advancement, high adventure, personal development and service. Explorer Scouting, for young men and women aged 14 through 20, concentrates on recreational activities and career awareness. Cub Scouting begins at six.

Girl Scouts

All Girl Scout programs are administered locally by area Councils. The Council for your region is listed in your area telephone book.

Girl Scout program activities are designed specifically to meet girls' needs. Activities include career exploration, outdoor education, substance abuse prevention and service to local communities. For girls aged 5 to 17.

Federation of Jewish Philanthropies

The Federation of Jewish Philanthropies sponsors day camps, overnight camps, study programs and trips to Israel. Your local synagogue and/or Jewish Community Center also have programs for young people.

Little League   (203) 585-5137

> Contact: Don Soucy
> P.O. Box 2926
> Bristol, CT 06011

Organized baseball for children aged 5 to 18. Little League Baseball and The Department of Health and Human Services are sponsoring a national bicycle safety program for 1994 along with CNA Insurance. Little League continues to distribute information about the dangers of smoking, drinking, drugs and chewing tobacco to 2.7 million children.

National 4-H Council   (301) 961-2853

> All 4-H programs are administered locally through the Cooperative Extension Service. The 4-H office for your community is listed in your area telephone book.

4-H is the largest informal education program in the United States. It serves children aged 9-19. Members carry out programs each year including planting projects, cooking, bike safety and peer group leadership.

Young Life

> International Service Center
> 720 W. Monument/P.O. Box 520
> Colorado Springs, CO 80901-0520

Young Life provides relaxed evenings with skits, conversation, and Christian religious discussion, as well as supervised trips. Outreach is available for troubled youths. For youths grades 9 to 12.

Wild Life (Young Life Affiliate)

> International Service Center
> 720 W. Monument/P.O. Box 520
> Colorado Springs, CO 80901-0520

Wild Life is a Young Life affiliated program tailored to the needs of middle school and junior high school students. Programs include skits, Christian religious discussion and supervised trips.

YMCA of the USA   **(214) 386-9622**

101 North Wacker Drive
Chicago, Illinois 60606

YMCA programs promote positive behavior in teens. Although programs vary from community to community, many provide teen leadership clubs, youth and government clubs, adventure programs, employment services and volunteer and mentorship opportunities. Physical activities include swimming, camping, health and fitness training and outdoor activities. Consult the telephone book for the YMCA nearest you.

YWCA of the USA   **(212) 614-2700**

726 Broadway
New York, NY 10003

YWCA programs vary, but most provide swimming, lifesaving, scuba, dancing, tennis, gymnastics, cooking, art, woodworking, badminton, volleyball and summer day camps.

Financing Community Projects

You will need financing to establish most of the programs and projects mentioned on the previous pages. Every town has sources you can turn to for financial help. But before approaching any source, think your project through. Then prepare a written presentation which outlines the program, lists fees, salaries, and overhead costs and states its objective.

Once you have the presentation, you will be better equipped to approach any of the following sources:

- **State and Federal congressmen and senators.** Government money is available for substance abuse prevention programs. Ask your representatives for help in applying for it.

- **Foundations.** Your local library should have a copy of The Foundation Directory, which lists foundations by state and shows their assets and the causes they support. Try to find a foundation in your area interested in adolescents and substance abuse prevention.

- **Area corporations.** Most corporations take an interest in substance abuse prevention and put money aside to fund prevention programs. Contact the companies in your area; and if you know an employee, work through him/her.

- **United Way.** The United Way supports programs which work to solve social problems. Call your local chapter and ask how to apply for United Way funding.

- **Residents.** Invite people in your community who can afford to sponsor your projects to join your board. Ask them to network among their friends to solicit contributions.

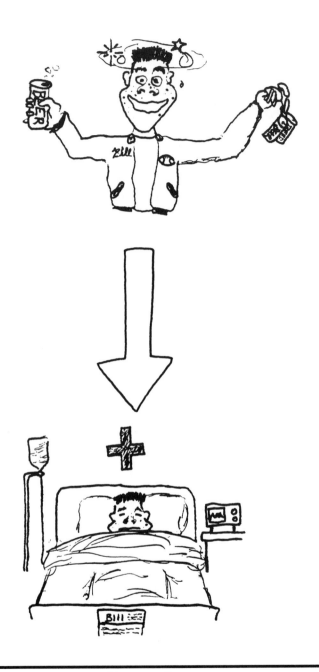

"If you're smart, you'll see when a party is getting out of hand and you'll get out." A high school sophomore.

Party Guidelines*

To teenagers, partying often connotes a large gathering of kids, invited and uninvited, in a home where parents are not present and where alcohol and drugs are. These are the notorious 'keg' parties, a part of the adolescent landscape despite the grim statistics on teenage drinking and driving. The majority of teenage fatalities occur in alcohol-related car crashes involving youths returning from late-night partying. If we reduce the number of unsupervised parties, we reduce the risk of losing our children, and there is a way to do that. Chaperoned parties can be successful gatherings without drugs or alcohol. Since socializing is as important and natural to a teenager as breathing, as parents we need to provide the arena for them to have fun in a safe and constructive way. **Below are party guidelines which we hope will help parents take an effective stand on social gatherings.**

If Your Child Is Attending a Get-together

1. Obtain the telephone number and address of the gathering and ask your teenager to call if there is a location change. Let your teen know where you can be reached at all times. It's a two-way street.

2. Call the host parent to be sure that it's a bonafide party and that an adult will be there.

3. Coordinate transportation to and from with your teen and other parents.

4. For teens of driving age, know who will be driving your teenager to and from the party. Ask your teen to contact you if there is a change in plans and he is not coming home directly.

5. Let your teen know that if he/she wishes to leave a party for any reason, including the presence of alcohol or drugs, he/she can call you or another designated adult.

6. Anticipate situations which might occur at parties and discuss specific ways of handling them with your teen.

7. Include your teenagers in gatherings where they can see adults having a good time without alcohol.

* Reprinted with permission of Parents Together, Greenwich, CT

If Your Child Is Hosting a Get-together

"My mother and I spent two weeks arguing about how often she and dad would walk through my party. We finally settled on every 15 minutes."

— A 14 year-old girl.

1. Plan the activity with your teen and make a guest list.

2. Encourage small informal gatherings. For larger parties, invitations discourage gate-crashers.

3. Specify what time the party will start and end.

4. Plan your event around skating, swimming, a rented movie, a sporting event, a cookout or a theme.

5. Notify your neighbors in advance as a courtesy.

6. For a large party, consider hiring an off-duty policeman to help guests park and discourage 'crashers'.

7. Consider co-hosting with other parents.

8. Discuss ground rules with your teen and decide how to convey these rules to guests.

9. Agree on the rules. For example:
   – No alcohol or drugs
   – No leaving the party and returning
     (teens sometimes leave drugs or alcohol outside)
   – No gate-crashers
   – Only one entrance and exit
   – Define which areas are off-limits (garage, yard, your child's room)
   – Drivers must put car keys on key rack

10. Have an adult at the door to greet and say 'good-bye' to guests.

11. Circulate. Circulate. Circulate. This is a very uncomfortable thing to do. Put on a big smile and do it anyway!

Parent-Teen Cooperation Is Vital

"When I come home at night the rule is I have to go up and kiss my mom goodnight. Often I sit on the edge of the bed and we talk awhile."

— A male high school senior.

1. Always know where to reach each other by phone.

2. Be awake (or ask to be awakened) when your teenager comes in at night.

3. Don't hesitate to set a curfew. Suggested ending times for teen events have been:

> 7th grade - 10:00 p.m.
> 8th grade - 10:30 p.m.
> 9th grade - 11:00 p.m.
> High School - 11:30 p.m. - 12:30 a.m.

Three times as many fatal alcohol-related car crashes occur at night as during the day. (The risk of being hit by a drunk driver increases late at night due to bar closings). (1)

"We only invited a few friends," they said.
"We don't know where all the others came from
and we couldn't make them leave. It got out of hand."

Hire a Sitter*

Mr. and Mrs. Goodparent live in a house in the suburbs with their two daughters who are 16 and 18 years old. Now and then the Goodparents like to go away on weekends and, at the girls urging, they decided some time ago that the girls were old enough to stay by themselves. They felt the house was in good hands and were happy to save the money that would otherwise go to a sitter.

They believed this until a month ago when they returned home from a weekend away to find tire ruts in their lawn, beer cans in their crushed shrubbery, cigarette burns in the carpeting, graffiti on their walls and both daughters in tears.

"We only invited a few friends," they said. "We don't know where all the others came from and we couldn't make them leave. It got out of hand."

The Goodparents' repair bills exceeded $5000.

An increasing number of families tell the Goodparents' story. Some beer parties are carefully planned by kids knowing their parents are going away. Others occur spontaneously at homes where kids converge and no adult is there to control their behavior. Even the best-behaved children are afraid to chase away friends or call the police on them.

Facts

- In towns across America police report being called *every weekend* to break up rowdy teen gatherings.
- City and town hospitals report regularly treating teenagers who are toxic from alcohol and/or drug abuse.
- The 1994 survey of the Institute for Highway Safety reports that 5,413 teenagers died in single vehicle car crashes. The majority of these accidents happened at night.
- Parents who allow minors to party unattended or to drink alcoholic beverages in their homes can be held legally responsible for injury to guests. (See Legal Obligations, page 149.)

* Reprinted with permission of The Greenwich Council on Youth and Drugs.

- School officials, police and others who work with adolescents believe that the number of unsupervised parties and nighttime car crashes would be drastically reduced if parents would make sure that their children are properly supervised while they're away - in other words, would hire a house sitter! Your teen will try to discourage you from doing this. *Don't be daunted – this is essential.*

Where Do I Find a House Sitter

- **Private school teachers**
- **Public school teachers**
- **Church staff members**
- **Senior citizens**
- **Yellow Pages** - look under "Sitting Services"

Be sure that your sitter knows that you want him/her to call the police if unwanted 'guests' won't leave.
REMEMBER, IF THERE IS INJURY TO LIFE OR LIMB, YOU CAN BE HELD RESPONSIBLE. (See Legal Obligations, page 149.)

Suggestion: If the cost of a sitter is an issue, consider forming a child-sitting pool with your friends. Leave your children with friends when you go away. Take care of their children when they leave home.

28

If Your Child Comes Home Drunk—Once

If your child attends a party like the one described in the previous section, he or she may come home drunk. If so, there are certain things parents should do.

That Night You Need To...
- keep calm despite feelings of anger.
- find out what drugs or how much alcohol he or she has taken.
- call a doctor or take your child to an emergency room if he or she is sick, passed out or incoherent.
- check frequently during the night.
- discuss the situation and the punishment with your spouse. Tommorrow, your collective consistency is essential.
- err on the side of caution. Don't minimize the situation. If you even suspect you need help, get it.
- wait until the next day to talk to your child. Do not become abusive. What you say or do will be lost on your child while he or she is drunk.

The Next Day You Need To...
- make your child assume responsibility for his actions, including clean-up.
- have a talk with your child. Keep your emotions under control. If anger cuts off the conversation, you may not learn everything you need to.
- find out when, where, and with whom your child was drinking/drugging. How did they get the alcohol/drugs?
- consider getting your child to sign a written contract promising not to repeat the behavior and listing future expectations.
- consider the possibility that this was not the first time. Talk to the school health educator, guidance counselor or your clergy.

Problems

Statistics and Trends

Mind-altering drug use by college kids began in the 60's with marijuana and LSD. By the 70's, a more potent marijuana moved down to the high school population and teenagers used alcohol regularly, often with parental consent. Young people argued that if they were old enough to go to war, they were old enough to drink. Most states agreed and lowered the drinking age. In the late 70's, an even stronger strain of marijuana appeared on the streets, which teens smoked as cavalierly as they drank alcohol. Rock stars were openly using drugs on and off the stage, which gave the practice greater appeal. By the early 80's, adolescent alcohol and other drug use was epidemic. All states raised the legal drinking age to 21. Nevertheless, the late 80's and early 90's have seen an ever younger group of children using and abusing alcohol and drugs. As you can see from the chart below, teens feel drugs are easy to obtain. The statistics and trends on the following pages reveal the scope of substance abuse and its related problems.

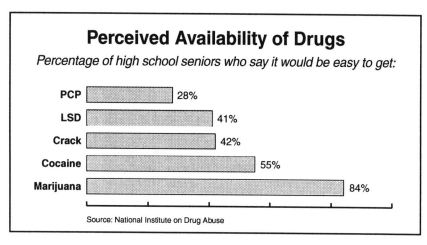

Teens Feel Drugs Are Easy to Obtain.

National Profile
of the American Adolescent

52% – aged 12 to 17 drink alcohol (1)

22.7% – aged 12 to 17 are drug involved (1)

55.8% – aged 18 to 25 are drug involved (1)

6% – have eating disorders (2)*

60% – 15 to 19 year-old males are sexually active (3)

50% – 15 to 19 year-old females are sexually active (3)

40% – become pregnant (3)

25% – suffer familial alcoholism (4)

35% – live in a family of divorce (5)

---

* Of the 6% who have eating disorders, 1% are anorexic and 5% are bulimic. Most eating disorder patients in this group are college aged. (2) However, the obsession with weight loss, fat and exercise can begin much earlier and go unrecognized as a problem for some time.

Please Note: Numbers in parentheses in this *Problems* section are keyed to the numbered list of statistical reference materials which begins on page i.

Alcohol and Other Drug Use

General Statistics:

- 35% of all wine coolers sold in the U.S. are sold to children in grades 7 through 12. (6)

- Use of alcohol, a gateway drug, usually precedes other drug use. Surveys show that teens who don't use alcohol use few or no drugs. Virtually no alcohol, tobacco or drug use begins after the age of 25. (7)

- Tobacco is the most heavily-promoted commercial product in America and the most lethal. Smoking kills more than 1,000 people each day. (8)

- Among adolescent cocaine users, 44% have sold drugs to support their habit, 31% have stolen from friends and family and 14% have attempted suicide. (9)

- 6.6% of U.S. male high school seniors have used steroids. (10)

- 15-20% of our children will be classified as serious substance abusers before they leave their teens. (11)

- Of the high school seniors who are daily users of marijuana, two-thirds of them began the pattern of use before the tenth grade. (12)

- By their late twenties, over 80% of today's young adults have tried an illicit drug. (12)

School Surveys:

57% of all illicit drugs are sold on school grounds and campuses from the sixth grade through college. (1)

Elementary School

- 25% of all fourth-graders in the U.S. are being pressured by their peers to try alcohol and other drugs. (2)
- Illegal drug and alcohol use is rising fastest in the 9 to 13 year-old age group. (3)

Middle School

- The chart below, which compares middle school use from 1991 to 1994, shows alcohol and other drug use steady or increasing among 6th to 8th graders. In previous years abuse among middle schoolers had been declining.

6th-8th Grade Students Who Use Drugs - 1991 to 1994			
Reprinted with permission of PRIDE (The Parents' Resource Institute for Drug Education, Atlanta, GA)			
	1991/1992	1992/1993	1993/1994
Cigarettes	25.2	25.5	26.3
Alcohol	41.1	41.0	40.0
Liquor	21.4	21.5	21.4
Marijuana	4.8	5.8	8.2
Cocaine	1.5	1.6	1.9
Uppers	3.0	3.0	3.4
Downers	2.2	2.2	2.4
Inhalants	4.8	4.8	5.9
Hallucinogens	1.8	1.9	2.1

- The national average age of first drug use is now 12. (4)
- 30% of male 13 year-olds and 22% of female 13 year-olds classify themselves as 'drinkers'. (5)
- Students as young as 12 report being able to buy alcohol without being 'carded'. (6)

High School

- Some 25% of U.S. high school seniors use drugs other than alcohol at least monthly. (7)

- Nearly a third of high school seniors believe there's no great risk in having four or five drinks almost every day. (8)

- In a 1993/94 PRIDE survey, when asked 'How many of your friends use beer?', only 13.7% of high school seniors said 'none.' 30.7% said 'most' of their friends drank beer. 27.4% said 'several' and 28.2% said 'a few'. (9)

High School Seniors Who Have Used Drugs

	1992	1994
Marijuana	33%	38.2%
Cocaine	6%	5.9%
Stimulants	14%	15.7%
Inhalants	17%	17.7%
Tranquilizers*	6%	6.6%
LSD	9%	10.5%
Narcotics	6%	6.6%

*Use of these drugs under doctor's orders is not included.
Source: U. of Michigan Surveys

College

- Binge drinking (five or more drinks in a row) is now a regular occurrence among 43% of all U.S. college students. 50% of college males report having five or more drinks in a row over the previous four weeks vs. 34% of college females. (10)

- Between 240,000 and 360,000 of the current college student population will eventually die of alcohol-related deaths such as liver disease. (10)

- 62.5% of 21–22 year old males and females have used an illicit drug. (10)

Suicide, Crime, Sex and Eating Disorders

- An average of 14 teens kill themselves every day. (1)

- Nearly half the teens who commit suicide are 'high' or drunk shortly before their deaths. (2)

- 8.3% of high school students have actually attempted suicide.(3)

- 31.5% of all male high school students report carrying weapons. 55.2% of the weapons carried are knives and razors. 24% are clubs and 20.8% are firearms. (3)

- By 12th grade, 76.3% of males and 66.6% of females have had sexual intercourse. (3)

- Nearly one-quarter of high school female students have induced vomiting to control their weight. (3)

- 34% of high school girls consider themselves to be 'fat.' (3)

- 28.3% of female high school seniors have used non-prescription diet pills. (4)

- More than half of college students who committed violent crimes said they were 'high' or drunk when they broke the law. (5)

Trends and Insights

Recent studies and interviews with police and social workers reveal certain trends developing among American youths —

- Recent surveys have consistently indicated that *suburban white students are using significantly more drugs*, especially alcohol, marijuana and LSD, than inner city black and Hispanic teens. A 1991 New York State survey showed that roughly twice as many suburban and rural white youths as inner city ethnic youths were using such drugs, a ratio which seems to hold up nationally. (1)

- *Alcohol is being consumed by younger and younger children* and many people believe media advertising is responsible. 23.7% of 6th graders drink beer. (2)

- Many doctors and scientists believe that *marijuana causes serious brain damage* and expect that research now in progress will prove this conclusively.

- *Steroid use is growing and probably underreported.* Professionals believe that in some areas as many as 25% of high school males are on steroids. More than a few are using them not only to compete better but also to improve their looks. Some athletes who used them in the 1970's now have cancer. The late NFL star, Lyle Alzado, and his doctors blamed his terminal cancer on his use of steroids and the Human Growth Hormone (HGH).

- *Inhalant use is on the rise,* according to the National Institute on Drug Abuse. Young teens, especially, are sniffing glue, gasoline and metallic paints and inhaling spray from aerosol products and some die using inhalants.

- Most of the increase in *female sexual activity in the 1980's was among white teenagers* and those in *higher income families.* (3)

- Contrary to what many people think, *teenage girls are using drugs virtually as much as teenage boys.* 22% of girls compared to 23.4% of boys aged 12 to 17 have used illicit drugs. (4)

- *Cities are seeing an increase in crack use and the formation of teenage gangs,* some members as young as 13. In some areas, homicide has replaced suicide as the second leading cause of death in teenagers, and in some cities it is the number one cause.

- It has become popular for teens to attend *parties called 'raves'.* A rave is an dance marathon attended by partygoers who often wear psychedelic jumpsuits. The object is to keep partying all night which partygoers achieve by taking drugs, usually hallucinogens. Raves began in England, but the English cracked down on them because a number of people died after taking Ecstasy. (5)

- *Adolescent treatment is becoming a priority in many communities.* A growing number of in-patient treatment centers, out-patient counselors and support groups are available to assist parents and their children in the often long-term process of recovery.

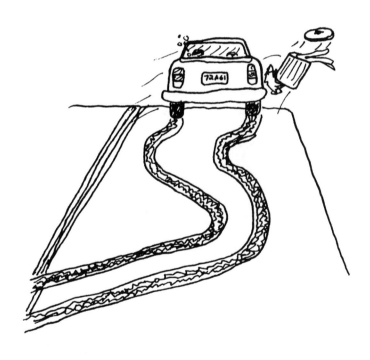

Drinking and driving is the #1 killer of teenagers. (1)

Alcohol Related Accidents, Sobering Statistics

Highway Accidents

Virtually any amount of alcohol will impair driving ability. Alcohol's effect is magnified by emotions, a run-down physical condition or use of medication or other drugs.

- The National Highway Traffic Safety Administration estimates 250 thousand persons were killed in alcohol-related crashes over the last ten years. (2)

- Teenage drivers with impaired blood alcohol content (BACs of .05 and above) are 54 times more likely to be killed in single vehicle crashes than sober teens. (2)

- Drivers aged 16-24 represent 17% of all licensed drivers, but 36% of all fatal alcohol-related car crashes. (3)

- In one year, 48% of 16-20 year old fatalities were in alcohol-related car crashes. (4)

Off-the-road Accidents

The majority of all accidents – not just auto – are caused by alcohol and other drugs.

- Each year, alcohol contributes to about 6 million non-fatal accidents and 15,000 fatal injuries at home, at play and in public places. (5)

- As many as 64% of recreational boating deaths are linked to alcohol. (6)

- Up to 40% of industrial fatalities and 47% of industrial accidents are alcohol-related. (7)

- 53% of falls, 38% of drownings and 64% of fires and burns are alcohol-related. (8)

41

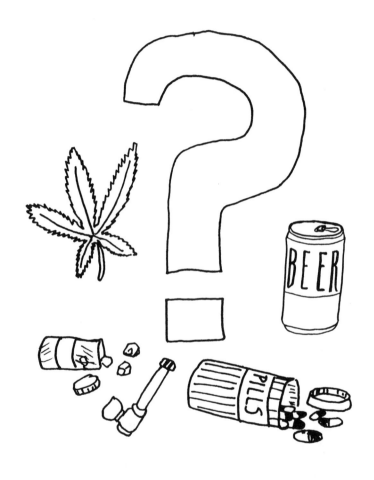

Teens turn to alcohol and other drugs for many reasons. They can be as simple as peer pressure or media influence; or they can run the gamut from low self-esteem to debilitating family problems.

Why Drugs and Alcohol?

Why do our children want to drink, smoke and take drugs? The reasons are complex and varied. Your child may be influenced by one or a few or many of the causes listed below:

Peer Pressure: There is seemingly nothing more important to teens than their peers. Every adolescent wants to be popular with his/her friends. If alcohol and other drugs make a child more acceptable to peers, it's often hard for a teen to say 'no'.

Low Self-Esteem: A common problem with alcohol use and drug abuse, this feeling of being less-than-good is often a reason for substance abuse.

To Escape: Adolescence is an uncomfortable and often painful time of life. Young people very often cannot live with uncomfortable feelings. As a society we have not been conditioned to understand that both 'good' and 'bad' feelings are normal and are better faced directly.

Drug-oriented Society: Adolescents are bombarded by television programs and commercials that promote drug use. Our children grow up with messages at home and in the media that no matter what the ailment, it can be 'fixed' with a drink or a pill. Alcohol is often glamorized in our culture. Before turning 18 the average child will see 75,000 drinking scenes on television programs. (1)

To Overcome Nervousness: Adolescents often feel insecure and shy, especially socializing with the opposite sex. Alcohol and other drugs loosen inhibitions and make teens feel relaxed and confident.

Failure: Every person needs to experience the feeling of success. Failure threatens a person's confidence, self-esteem and self-respect. To compensate, many young people find their 'success' in the dream world of alcohol and other drugs where failure is forgotten — for as long as the 'high' lasts.

Affluence and Permissiveness: Indulgent parents make it hard for their children to accept discipline and limitations. Parents give children money without making them accountable for it. Often children will spend such money on alcohol, drugs and rock music of the kind described below.

Boredom: Many adolescents are not involved in enough productive activities in their lives. Lack of purpose leads to a search for excitement, thrills and challenge.

Depression: Whenever there is chronic depression in the family — or on the part of the teen — there is a tendency for the adolescent to want to block out the painful feelings with alcohol or other drugs.

Availability: Availability of alcohol and drugs in home medicine cabinets and liquor cabinets makes usage all too easy for teenagers. Illegal drugs are sold right on school grounds and professional drug dealers work within walking distance of countless schools.

Unresolved Family Problems: If adolescents come from homes where serious problems are not addressed, they often drink or use drugs to escape.

Curiosity: Young people hear about 'highs' and want to find out for themselves. They wonder what it feels like. Getting 'high' is often glamorized in the lyrics of popular music, and this piques a teen's curiosity.

To Assert Independence: Drinking is seen as adult behavior. Teens feel that by drinking they are part of the adult world.

Parent Role Models: Adolescents who see parents and other adults drinking and/or smoking often imitate the behavior.

Genetic Predisposition: Many studies show that children with an alcoholic parent are at much higher risk of becoming alcoholic themselves. Furthermore, they are likely to become dependent at a young age.

Rebellion Against Authority: Some teens drink and do drugs to disobey authority. They're ready to fight any rules set for them, at home, at school and in society.

Absence of Standards: The failure of many families to establish and maintain consistent moral and ethical standards has unfortunately led to many young people becoming involved in unacceptable behavior. Parents who tell the truth set a standard for honesty; who drink moderately and encourage alcohol-free partying with children set a standard for responsible drinking; who don't smoke, swear and who observe speed limits set good examples for their children to emulate.

Invulnerability: Young people often feel that they're indestructible and therefore see no danger in alcohol and other drugs, even though they are taught otherwise.

Sports Celebrity Role Models: When prominent athletes promote alcohol or are publicized as drug users it sends a strong message to kids that doing drugs is cool.

Abuse: Abuse in the family — physical, verbal, emotional or sexual — often leads to chemical dependency as a way of escaping the emotional pain.

Rock Music: According to Parents Music Resource Center in Arlington, VA, children spend on average 11,000 hours listening to rock music from 6th grade to 12th (2). Much rock music is fun, but some glorifies drinking, drugging, bondage, sado-masochism and violence against females. Parents should monitor the music their children listen to.

"*While we looked the other way, a mutant strain of rock developed advocating drug use, casual sex and sado-masochism.*"

Rock and Rap

Rock 'n Roll

Those of us who were around in the early days of rock 'n roll remember 'slow-dancing' to 3-minute love songs, such as *'Smoke Gets in Your Eyes'* or *'The Great Pretender',* or twisting to goofy songs like *'Alley Oop'* and *'Get A Job'* whose lyrics Steve Allen used to read on his show to make us laugh.

As rock evolved, however, the music seemed to become louder and the lyrics less comprehensible. Many of us who were rock's early fans tended to tune out and ignore the new sound as we busied ourselves with parenting and building careers. While we looked the other way, a mutant strain of rock developed advocating drug use, casual sex and sado-masochism. Not surprisingly, this new hard-core genre caught on quickly with the thrill-seeking teenage set.

The Parents Music Resource Center (PMRC) in Arlington, Virginia has produced an excellent video which identifies five recurring themes in hard-core rock and offers examples of each. The themes are:

1. *Aggressive Rebellion* —

- *Twisted Sister* produced a video to accompany its song *'We're Not Going To Take It Anymore'* which shows a teen in his room playing his guitar when his father enters the room and yells at him to get to work. The teen flies into a rage and throws his father through a plate-glass window.

- Gene Simmons, the lead singer of the group *Kiss,* said in an interview "People are going to tell you can't do this, you can't do that. They can all go f__ themselves collectively and that includes your parents."

2. *Abuse of Alcohol and Drugs* —

- The lead singer of *Motley Crue* was convicted of killing the drummer of a rival band and critically injuring two other people while driving drunk. Afterwards his message to his fans was it's fun "to be f__d up. Drink, shoot up heroin, do whatever you want, just don't drink and drive."

3. *Graphic Violence and Suicide* —

- The parents of John McCollum sued *Ozzy Osborne* because their son killed himself while listening to Osborne's record 'Suicide Solution'. The McCollum family lost the suit. Steve Boucher killed himself while listening to *AC DC's* album *'Shoot to Thrill'*.

- Street gangs identify with particular rock groups. They tend to choose those with the most violent messages and play their music wherever the gang congregates. (See Gangs, page 118.)

4. *Fascination with the Occult* —

- A group called *Venom* is one of several groups that glorify satanism. They detail satanic rituals in their music and their lyrics "demand...the death of God."

5. *Sexuality Which is Graphic and Explicit* —

- The behavior of a nymphomaniac is detailed in a song in *Prince's 'Purple Rain'* album; and sister/brother incest is the subject of a song in his *'Dirty Mind'* album.

- Bondage, body excretions and how much fun the pain of love can be are the subject of Mick Jagger's *'The Pain of Love'*.

- *The Mentors*, in *'Golden Showers'*, sing of excrement, flatulation and a woman's face becoming their 'toilet paper'.

Any 8 year-old can go into the local record store and buy songs like the ones mentioned above.

To obtain the PMRC's excellent video and their 'Let's Talk Rock' handbook or to get more information about rock music, call or write:

The Parents Music Resource Center
1500 Arlington Boulevard
Arlington, Virginia 22209
Tel. (703) 527-9466

Rap

Rap, which is basically rhyme spoken to music, sprang from 'hip-hop' which gained popularity in New York in the late 70's. By the late 80's, rap like rock had its shock-value version popular with thrill-seeking youths. The relatively new hard-core rap is known as 'Gangsta Rap' and two themes recur throughout it. They are:

1. *Violence born of a radical racial point of view —*
- In *'F_ The Police'*, N.W.A. (Niggas With Attitude) threaten that 'a nigger on the warpath' will create a 'bloodbath of cops dying in L.A.'
- In *'By the Time You Get to Arizona'*, *Public Enemy* sing that they are 'on the one mission to get a politician,' and one of the rappers claims to be a 'triggerman looking for the governor.' This was an expression of anger at the state of Arizona because it would not recognize the Martin Luther King holiday. The Arizona Governor at the time was in fact in favor of the holiday.
- The *Geto Boys* gleefully describe killing in their rap songs. Geto Boys' Brad Jordan sings of pulling out an anti-personnel shotgun known as a Streetsweeper and hitting three or four people in the head.
- In *'Black Korea'*, Ice Cube chants disrespectfully about Orientals and threatens to burn down a Korean's store.

2. *Sexual violence toward women —*
- 'If she wants it she's gonna bleed' sings *Guns and Roses* to a 'very sexy girl' in *'Welcome to the Jungle'*.
- Rappers *2 Live Crew* were forced to go to court in Florida to defend their right to sing songs about tearing open vaginas, slaying women 'rough and painful' and sodomizing women. They won.

- In *'Giving Up the Nappy Dug Out', Ice Cube* boasts of diddling a 14 year-old girl and warns her father that he'll become 'shotgun fodder' if he's got a problem with it.

Not surprisingly, Gangsta Rap has sparked serious social controversy. Rappers and the record companies that produce their songs argue that Gangsta Rap is simply a reflection of life as it is in the ghetto and an appeal for public sympathy. Opponents argue that it is just profit-driven sleaze that preys upon the emotions of disadvantaged Americans and incites violent and bestial behavior. The strongest backlash is in the Afro-American community itself where decent people are trying to curb violence, not encourage it.

Black women are particularly offended by the recurring images of themselves as sex objects who exist to be abused. Rappers argue that their songs are not responsible for any real life violence, but many disagree. Two disputed incidents follow:

- Ronald Ray Howard claimed in his own defense that he was listening to '2Pacalypse Now' (an album containing six songs with 'cop-killing' themes) when he shot and killed Texas state trooper Bill Davidson on April 11, 1992.

- A gang of youths were chanting the rap song phrase *'Whoomp, There It Is'* when they tore the bathing suit off a 14 year-old girl in a New York City public swimming pool. There were six such incidents in New York in July of 1993. The 'It' in the title refers to a girl's bare bottom. Of the incident, Joseph Simmons of *Run-DMC* said that parents have more to do with disrespect toward women than do rappers.

Rock Concerts

Rough behavior is not unusual at rock concerts and drug use is common. Consider the following:

- Two youths were crushed to death at a *Guns and Roses* concert by slam-dancing fans.
- Rapper Ice-T was quoted as saying "We don't have a good show unless an ambulance shows up."
- Drugs, particularly marijuana and LSD, are pushed at rock concerts.

What To Do About Rock and Rap

1. Write PMRC at the above address for information about groups your children listen to and get PMRC's list of record companies.
2. Write to record companies whose products offend you and get like-minded parents to write as well. Ask them to send you lyrics. If they don't comply, assume the lyrics are offensive.
3. Make your children accountable for the money you give them and be aware of what sort of music they are purchasing.
4. If your children listen to music you find offensive, discuss it with them. Suggest alternatives.

ROCK AND RAP

TV reinforces violent feelings in children who lead violent lives. (2)

The Media

Does TV increase violent behavior? Does it make people promiscuous? Do beer commercials encourage kids to drink? Do cigarette ads make kids smoke? Do fashion models promote bulimia? As the debate rages on, there is mounting evidence that media influence is strong, especially in children. The following may shed some light on the subject of media influence.

Television Violence

In June 1993, the United States Senate Subcommittees on the Constitution and Juvenile Justice held hearings to examine the influence of television violence on the nation's youth. It is not the first time the entertainment industry has come before Congress to answer for media content, but it is the first time that government officials have had an 'overwhelming' body of evidence to suggest that media violence does in fact encourage violent behavior in children who watch it.(1) Even the TV moguls present agreed that it might be so.

At the conclusion of the hearings the TV industry agreed to consider some sort of rating system. Government representatives, not quite satisfied with the industry's proposal, threatened to impose regulations on television if the industry refused to take the findings on violence seriously.

Four months following the hearings ABC aired a new show called *NYPD Blue* which brought raw violence, graphic sex and four-letter words to a major network for the first time.

Here are some interesting statistics and incidents concerning media and violence:

- On average, an American child sees 8000 murders and 100,000 acts of violence on TV before he leaves grade school. (1)

- TV reinforces violent feelings in children who lead violent lives. Children living in tough neighborhoods and lacking real-life role models imitate the behavior of gun-wielding TV heroes.(2)

- In the U.S. 270,000 children carry handguns into school each day.(2)

- TV glamourizes violence and desensitizes us to it. When heroes get severely wounded, they often keep going as if nothing has happened. Japan takes the opposite approach. Violence, where it occurs in Japanese fiction, is realistic. It affects someone the audience likes, raising sympathy for the victim and revulsion to the act. The homicide rate in the U.S. is 11 times that of Japan.(3)

- Children who are heavy viewers of TV act more aggressively than light viewers. Over-exposure to aggression teaches young people that it is the tool used to solve conflicts. (2)

- "The arrival of TV in South Africa coincided with a doubling of the murder rate," writes Brandon S. Centerwall in The Journal of the American Medical Association. A town in Canada called "Notel" by researchers experienced a rise in homicides soon after it acquired TV. Researchers also measured a 150% increase in aggression in "Notel's" children once they began watching TV. (1)

- Tens of millions of TV viewers watch MTV cable television The majority of MTV viewers are teenagers. Programming includes playing rock and rap songs as well as videos and features talk hosts and music news. In the early 90's, MTV added an animated feature called Beavis and Butthead. In October 1993 a baby girl was killed when her five year-old brother set fire to their home, an act which his mother said he learned to do from Beavis and Butthead. MTV agreed to review program content after the incident and to move the show to a later hour.

- Although some people question the extent to which the media contribute to violence in America, there is no question about which civilized nation is the most violent. The United States wins the race by many lengths as the chart below shows. (3)

Comparison of Homicide Rates
Males Aged 15 through 24

UNITED STATES	21.9
SCOTLAND	5.0
NEW ZEALAND	4.4
ISRAEL	3.7
NORWAY	3.3
FINLAND	3.0
CANADA	2.9
AUSTRALIA	2.5
SWEDEN	1.7
BELGIUM	1.4
NETHERLANDS	1.4
SWITZERLAND	1.4
FRANCE	1.4
GREECE	1.4
IRELAND	1.2
POLAND	1.2
ENGLAND & WALES	1.2
PORTUGAL	1.0
DENMARK	1.0
W. GERMANY	1.0
JAPAN	0.5
AUSTRIA	0.3

Homicides Per 100,000 Population

Advertising

TV successfully sells advertising time with the promise that TV advertising *will influence* countless numbers to go out and buy the advertiser's product. Advertisers clearly believe that ads and commercials 'sell soap' because they spend billions of dollars every year advertising their products. By contrast the television industry has, for a long time, claimed that its program content *does not influence* behavior. **Consider the following facts:**

- To attract advertisers, one television network ran a newspaper ad with the headline *Only Our Kids Have This Much Power Over Their Parents.* It went on to say that our children influence how we spend $130 billion a year and that kids themselves spend $8 billion. Advertisers count on our children to pester us into buying them junk-food, name-label clothing, toys and tapes. (1)

- Children see approximately 100,000 beer ads and commercials by the age of 21. Brewers say that they do not intend to condition our children, but research indicates that beer commercials have an impact on young minds. (2)

- 51% of teens tested matched an animal mascot with the particular brand of beer he promoted. This suggests that kids are paying close attention to the ads. (3)

- Reactions to beer commercials of teens tested were that "They make drinking beer look glamourous", "Drinking beer makes you look cool and accepted," and "They have sexy women." (3)

- Research suggests that alcohol and cigarette advertisers target poor inner city neighborhoods. In a 19-block stretch in Philadelphia, 56 out of 73 billboards advertised alcohol or cigarettes. In New Orleans, there were 515 billboards in a black district as opposed to 138 in an adjacent white one. 58% advertised alcohol and cigarettes. Studies done in Detroit, Boston, San Francisco and St. Louis found similar results.(5)

- An AAA study revealed that highly attentive young viewers of automobile commercials are far more likely to speed, swerve and take chances. (4)

- AAA's studies suggest that beer commercials equate masculinity with physical challenges, risky behavior, macho insensitivity, disregard of consequences and exploitation of one-dimensional females. Further, they present beer as the ultimate reward for work. Such images have an impact on suggestible adolescents, particularly when presented by sports idols. (4)

Packaging

Advertisers know that children spend $8 billion annually and they target the 'kid' market aggressively.

- Wine coolers are packaged to look like flavored spring water drinks. 61% of students tested could not tell the difference between a wine cooler bottle and one that held mineral water and juice. (3)

- Underground chemists who make LSD package it on blotter paper imprinted with cartoon characters and other symbols familiar to children.

- TV and print media have for years equated feminine beauty with thinness, using ultra-thin models to sell their products (Twiggy). The ideal of 'thinness' has produced a national obsession which has even grade school girls worried about their weight. One-third of all teenage girls experiment with purging to stay thin. In 1993, the fashion industry answered the concern over eating disorders by creating the 'waif' look using even younger, slighter models than they had in the past.

Should We Rely on Government or Ourselves to Shield Children from Exposure to Offensive Material in the Media?

It's a Big Problem

A couple of generations ago parents were not so concerned about the exposure of their children to offensive material in the media. Radio, movies, 78-rpm and "hi-fi" records, magazines, newspapers and books: those were "the media." And content was more tightly regulated. Movies had a voluntary code of self-censorship, while the Federal Communications Commission (which still acts for Congress to license use of the limited number of airwave frequencies) scrutinized radio program content. Mail order was in its infancy: records and print media were mostly sold in the neighborhood or kept on the shelves of school and local libraries, so that distribution was subject to community scrutiny.

Today, for better or worse, "the media" have expanded to include broadcast television, cable TV, video and cassette tapes, CD's and even computer online services and the Internet. All of these except the last have joined radio, the movies, records and print media in bombarding consumers young and old, inside and outside the home, with pervasive and unceasing demands for attention. The principle of voluntary self-censorship has been discarded or assigned a very low priority by media-oriented businesses. These days a parent who wants to block or restrict a child's access to offensive media messages faces a truly serious challenge.

The First Amendment and the Courts

If parents and voters want youngsters shielded from indecency and violence in the media, why didn't our lawmakers long ago pass laws providing such shelter? The answer is the First Amendment to our Constitution, which says that "Congress shall make no law ..... abridging the freedom of speech, or of the press."

The Federal courts, which interpret the First Amendment, have repeatedly applied it to limit or even prevent efforts by lawmakers and regulators to block or censor the expression of unpopular or controversial ideas and opinions. True, in protecting free expression the Constitution does not justify libel, or the betrayal of military secrets in wartime, or the grossest, most sickening kinds of obscenity, pornography or sado-masochism. But the courts have extended the protection of the First Amendment far beyond political issues to give business the right of commercial free speech and to shelter artistic expression. Bearing in mind that what's indecency to one person may be art to another, judges have again and again decided that almost any form of expression merits First Amendment protection if it is labelled as "artistic" by its creator, publisher or distributor. Media - oriented businesses have strong bottom-line financial reasons for supporting this approach.

Where adults are concerned Americans must accept as one of the "dilemmas of liberty" (1) this ongoing struggle between civil libertarians reluctant to accept any restraint on free expression and plain folk demanding a safe harbor or shelter from media messages which large number of Americans consider indecent, violent or otherwise offensive. But the media audience also includes children, and this changes the terms of the debate. House Speaker Newt Gingrich recently asked on the floor of Congress "How do you maintain the right of free speech for adults while also protecting children in a medium which is available to both?" Our courts are coming to agree that children need protection. For example, in mid-1995 a majority of the entire U.S. Court of Appeals for the D.C. Circuit, a key Federal court, decided that the Government has a "compelling interest" in shielding children from exposure to indecent material shown on broadcast television. (2)

Will Federal Laws Provide the Solution?

Whenever we talk with our readers and other interested people we find a strong tide of parental opinion condemning indecency and violence in the media. This tide has reached Congress as well as our Federal courts, perhaps because the 1994 elections brought so many new faces from the grass roots to Washington. As this edition goes to press each house of Congress has passed its own version of a landmark 1995 telecommunications bill that would regulate indecency and violence on television and possibly even in online services and on the Internet. The bills assume the makers of TV sets will be able to perfect and install so-called "V-chips" that, when used together with a not-yet-developed rating system, will enable parents to prevent their children from watching programs rated as unacceptable on indexes of indecency or violence. The authors wonder whether a chip/rating system easy enough for parents to use will be immune to deactivation or sabotage by children of the computer generation.

So what can we do while the courts and Congress grapple with these questions?

Practical Self-Help Suggestions

Parents as individuals have free speech rights too; and we can use these rights to crystallize and mobilize public opinion. America's economy is market-driven. Businesses will listen to parents and parent groups who send this message:

- Business has no obligation to test the outer limits of free speech.
- Business does have an obligation not to expose our children to indecency and violence.
- There will be an economic cost to the businesses that ignore this message.

How Do You Make Your Voice Heard?

Most of us have stationery and telephones. Many of us have access to fax machines. Many belong to church or temple discussion groups, or to other community and social organizations.

What messages can be sent? Parents and parental groups can and should do the following:

- Demand self-censorship by those who now profit by exploiting material that is offensive to contemporary community standards.
- Alert entertainment media to their moral/ethical responsibility to the community not to produce or distribute films, programs or songs that contain indecent or violent scenes, dialog or lyrics.

- Contact the businesses that sponsor or support such films or programs to say that you have stopped using their products or services, and why.
- Contact bookstores, music shops and others to urge as a parent that they choose not to deal in publications, records and tapes offensive to contemporary community standards; or that they at least restrict access to such materials to adults.
- Turn off offensive programs in your home, and discuss with your children why you have done so. Likewise, keep up to date on the kind of records and tapes they own, rent or exchange, and spot check the lyrics.
- Speak up in local meetings about the importance of shielding children from offensive material in media and publications.
- To beam the 'white light of publicity' on a persistent local problem, write letters to local newspapers and phone in to any local call-in radio program(s).

Remember, concerned parents are not blue-nosed censors, fanatics or fascists just because they turn off programs, refuse to buy products and services and complain to producers, distributors, retailers, sponsors and advertisers about offensive program content. Concerned parents are people who want to bring up their children in a wholesome environment. Don't let those who exploit our children for profit in the name of free speech deter you from exercising your own free speech rights.

"We ran out of pot. I'd never done acid. But my girlfriend told me, 'Look, it's no big deal, you'll get a buzz.' So, I tried it. I tried a lot of drugs after that and decided I liked heroin best." — 18 year-old girl.

Gateway Drugs:
Alcohol, Tobacco and Marijuana

Alcohol, cigarettes, smokeless tobacco and marijuana are the most abused drugs upon which a person can become dependent. Many people mistakenly believe that these drugs are harmless catalysts for fun. American culture aids and abets this attitude by heavily advertising alcohol and tobacco products and glamorizing their use in the movies. Far too little is said about the toll they have taken on American society. Addiction to any one of them destroys the user's health, affects the addict's school or job performance and wreaks havoc on his or her family.

Attitudes about alcohol, tobacco and marijuana need to change. When we, as parents, look to any one of them to alter our mood, we pass along the message to our children that they can look to drugs to make themselves feel better. When we say "Give me a drink, I need to relax," we are telling our children that a drink gets us through difficult times.

Tolerance to alcohol, tobacco or marijuana often leads people to search for other drugs in the quest to get 'high' quickly. This is why they are sometimes called 'Gateway Drugs'. For example, teenagers dust marijuana with PCP (called 'dusting') or dip it in formaldehyde (known as 'illy') for a greater 'kick'... two very dangerous practices. Teenagers who use marijuana frequently interact with teens who are using other drugs and are lured into using them as well.

With all three of these substances, the immature teenage body becomes addicted far more quickly than an adult body. It takes an adult 5 – 15 years to become addicted to alcohol, while a teenager can become addicted in 6 months to 2 years. And addiction in a teenager is far more difficult to reverse than in an adult. The following pages detail the harmful effects of alcohol, tobacco and marijuana.

Alcohol

"I started drinking Fridays and Saturdays at keg parties. Pretty soon, it was every day. I sipped vodka from ginger ale cans at school and hid it on my dresser in perfume bottles."
— *Recovering 18 year-old girl*

A 1992 survey of high school seniors found that 32.2% had consumed 5 or more drinks in a row in the two weeks prior to the survey.(1)

As the statistic above suggests, binge drinking has become a rite of passage for American youth. Today, there are grade school children who drink more than once a week and the average age at which adolescents first get drunk is 12. Illicit alcohol use is rising fastest among middle schoolers. **A Harvard study reveals that:**

- **47.9% of college men admit to 'binge' drinking.**
- **21.2% of college women admit to 'binge' drinking.**

By their senior year in high school, nearly one-third of all teens binge drink. In high school and college, chug-a-lug beer games go on for hours and funneling is especially popular. A plastic tube is attached to a funnel and the opposite end of the tube is inserted in the throat. The plastic is clamped, the funnel is filled with an alcoholic beverage, the clamp is released and the alcohol pours into the stomach.

The net result in so much early and excessive drinking in adolescence is that doctors and treatment professionals are seeing an epidemic increase in the number of alcoholics in the teenage and young adult years. Alcoholics Anonymous reports that programs have been established from coast to coast for teenagers and adults in their early 20's. These programs are relatively new because there simply was no need for them in decades past.

There are strong connections between heavy drinking and other destructive behavior in teens. Alcohol slows reflexes, impairs cognition, changes moods and suppresses inhibitions. An intoxicated person may therefore act out behavior he or she would normally only think about. The Harvard study mentioned above reveals that roughly one-third of the students interviewed said they experienced an unplanned sexual activity after heavy drinking. Nearly 18% of the males in the study damaged property while binge drinking and 9.1% got into trouble with the police.(2) Young girls who feel pressured into sex have said "I have to drink to do it." Some say they drink to forget what they did the night before because it's hard to look themselves in the mirror the next morning. Half of those who commit crimes claim as their defense that they were under the influence of alcohol. Psychologists believe that heavy drinking can lead a youth to act on suicidal feelings.

In light of the above, parents who condone teenage drinking and support programs which claim to promote 'safe drinking' for teens may want to rethink this issue. Programs which discourage teens from drinking and driving under the influence are laudable. But driving accidents are only one consequence of drinking. The potential for alcoholism, alcohol poisoning, accidents and violence suggests that a no use message is better than one that suggests it's O.K. to drink as long as you don't drive.

Appeal — Users experience loss of inhibitions and feel socially relaxed, especially with the opposite sex.

Harm — *Alcohol is a drug.* It is the most overused drug in America by all age groups. Most treatment professionals consider alcohol the greatest threat to our youth today. Why the concern? Because the immediate as well as long-term risks for using alcohol at a young age are significant. While it may take several years for adults to become dependent on alcohol, teenagers may become alcoholics in a matter of months. Continued use of alcohol damages and eventually destroys brain cells. Specifically, it attacks a group of cells crucial in memory formation. Thus, heavy users frequently suffer blackouts, time periods when the user appears to be functioning but has no memory of what has happened. Long-term memory is affected as well. Studies indicate that alcohol affects the function of the frontal lobe first, impairing one's sense of values and self-awareness.

Drinking any alcohol can lead to alcoholism, which is an incurable disease. Although this chronic disease is not curable, it is treatable. Alcoholism presents many life-threatening medical hazards such as cirrhosis of the liver, gastric ulcers, gastritis, degeneration of the cerebellum — to name a few. There is increased risk of cancer if the drinker also smokes. Alcohol also promotes cancer of the lungs, pancreas, esophagus, intestines and the prostate.

Alcohol poisoning kills at least 400 teens annually.(3) After graduating from high school, an 18 year-old girl drank tequila at an "all you can drink for $5 party" and passed out. Her sister took her home and put her to bed and she died in her sleep. An autopsy revealed that her blood alcohol level was .38%. (People are legally drunk at .10%). A 17 year-old boy died in a similar way when friends funneled bourbon into his stomach and left him to sleep it off.

Tragedy does not necessarily spare the teen who "is only having a couple of beers with friends." A young person who has had just two drinks is far more likely to have a traffic accident than an adult who has had two drinks.(4) Parents need to teach respect for the law and they need to emphasize that drinking under the age of 21 is illegal.

Some adolescents have been known to drink head cold and cough medications which contain as much as 25% alcohol, as well as vanilla extract which can be as high as 35% alcohol. *Parents need to be aware of what's on their shelves and in their medicine cabinets.*

WHAT TO LOOK FOR: Alcohol hidden in cologne bottles or other containers, watered down or missing alcohol from the liquor cabinet.

SIGNS OF USE: Slurred speech, odor of alcohol, balance problems, blackouts.

COST: $4.29 for a 4-pack wine cooler. $4.00-$5.00 for a 6-pack of beer. Keg of beer, $70 to $75.

LENGTH OF ALCOHOL HIGH: Variable. Generally it takes the body one hour to metabolize one ounce of liquor.

FAS (Fetal Alcohol Syndrome) — Teen pregnancy has reached epidemic proportions, and there is a strong link between teen pregnancy and Fetal Alcohol Syndrome (FAS). FAS is the term given to a pattern of mental, physical, and behavioral defects which appear in the children of mothers who drank during pregnancy. As many as 5% of all birth defects may be attributable to prenatal alcohol exposure. (5) The Department of Health and Human Services lists FAS as the leading cause of mental retardation. The National Council on Alcoholism and Drug Dependence perceives any alcohol consumption during pregnancy as high-risk drinking and supports a clear no-alcohol use message.

ALCOHOL

67

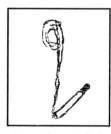

Cigarettes

The American Cancer Society estimates that cigarette smoking is responsible for 85% of lung cancer cases among men and 75% among women. Smoking accounts for about 30% of all cancer deaths.

Appeal — Adolescents think smoking makes them more grown up.

Harm — Tobacco smoking kills more Americans than AIDS, heroin, crack, cocaine, alcohol, car accidents, fire and murder combined. Cigarette smoke is not a localized toxin. It affects the whole body, damaging the heart, the circulatory system and the skin, and is responsible for a high incidence of bladder cancer. Because nicotine is a highly addictive substance, the cigarette habit is hard to break. Tobacco is just as addictive as alcohol, heroin and other drugs which work to 'hook' the user.

With teenagers, cigarette smoking usually precedes the use of marijuana and other drugs. Chronic tobacco use is closely associated with other drug use. The latest report states that 84% of marijuana users are using tobacco and 89% of cocaine users are also smokers. (1) Therefore, prevention of cigarette smoking is a high priority in the prevention of drug dependence.

Our children are educated in school about the dangers of smoking and, in addition, the American Cancer Society's program "Cigarette Smoking: Take It Or Leave It" is available to help teens make up their own minds about the risks of smoking.

WHAT TO LOOK FOR: Matches in pockets, hidden packs of cigarettes, burn holes in clothes, cigarette butts extinguished in empty bottles, smell of cigarette smoke.

SIGNS OF USE: Smoker's breath, hacking cough, frequent colds, raspy hoarse voice.

COST: $2.35 per pack.

Smokeless Tobacco

21.9% of teen males in the United States, aged 12-17, have used smokeless tobacco. (1)

Sales of smokeless tobacco products have risen dramatically since 1964 despite the U.S. Surgeon General's report on their carcinogenic properties and the danger they pose to health. In 1980 snuff dipping and tobacco chewing were again popular among baseball players. This started a craze for 'dipping' among teenage boys in the suburbs. At that time television commercials showed famous sports figures promoting chewing tobacco.

Smokeless tobacco is snuff, chewing or plug tobacco. Dipping is the practice of placing a pinch of snuff between the lower lip and teeth where it mixes with the saliva and is absorbed. Dipping is a favorite among male adolescents. Chewing tobacco is loose tobacco that is sold in a pouch and is placed between the cheek and the gum. Tobacco can also be bitten from a solid plug and chewed.

Appeal — Adolescent males believe it's 'macho'.

Harm — Dipping tobacco is extremely hazardous because it mixes with saliva and is absorbed by the body. The smokeless tobacco by-products are especially irritating to the delicate tissues inside the mouth. They can cause cancer of the pharynx, cancer of the cheek and lip, and leukoplakia, a pre-cancerous condition caused by irritation.

Dangers to other organs include arteriosclerosis, stomach ulcers, heart attacks, cancer of the esophagus, the larynx and the bladder.

WHAT TO LOOK FOR: Dark brown liquid (which users spit out in glasses or cups) and little round tins, similar to shoe wax tins, but slightly smaller.

SIGNS OF USE: Decayed teeth, ground down teeth, gum infection, bleeding mouth sores, a persistently red or white palate, difficulty in chewing or moving jaws, thickening of mouth tissue.

COST: $2.30 per tin.

Marijuana (Cannabis)

"You get hooked on pot real bad and you want it. And you keep needing it and your body wants it and you'd do anything to get the money for it."

— Teenager quoted in *Teen Drug Use.*

Marijuana (cannabis sativa) is known as grass, joint, pot and weed. Parts of the plant can be smoked or eaten to alter the state of the user. Parents who experimented with marijuana in the 70's tend to think the drug is harmless. However today, the mind-altering ingredient in marijuana, tetrahydrocannabinol (THC), is cultivated to a *potency which is 470% stronger in 1993 than it was in 1974.* (1) Hashish (hash) is the pure resin extracted from the cannabis sativa plant, usually with an even higher THC potency than grass, and is smoked in small pipes. Hash use is marked by faster heartbeat and pulse rate, dry mouth and throat and bloodshot eyes.

Marijuana is usually bought in small plastic baggies called 'nickel' or 'dime' bags. One ounce of marijuana will make approximately 40 to 50 joints (marijuana cigarettes.) Adolescents can also buy joints individually, which is what the youngest teens tend to do.

Appeal — Users feel socially relaxed, comfortable. Mildly hypnotic, makes user 'spaced out'.

Harm — Many people believe that marijuana is harmless and even medicinal. In fact, a strong pro-legalization lobby has petitioned the government repeatedly over the years to legalize the drug on claims that it is a powerful anti-nauseant and it alleviates glaucoma symptoms. But each time the government has denied the petition because it believes the drug is harmful. At hearings held in March of 1992, the government argued that there are anti-nauseants on the market, including one derived from THC, which are highly effective and don't have the side effects of smoking marijuana. Furthermore, marijuana can cause dramatic drops in the blood supply to the head and eyes which could speed up rather than slow down loss of eyesight.

In refusing the petition to legalize the Government cited evidence that marijuana —

- is even more likely to be *cancer-causing* than tobacco.

- damages *brain* cells.

- causes *lung problems* such as bronchitis and emphysema.

- may weaken the body's antibacterial *defenses* in the lungs.

- causes sudden drops in blood pressure, *rapid heart beat* and heart palpitations.

- affects the production of progesterone, an important *female hormone*.

- causes *anxiety* and *panic*.

- produces dizziness, *trouble with thinking*, concentrating.

- causes fatigue, sleepiness and *impairs motor skills*.

- harbors the bacteria *pathogenic aspergillus* which kills an estimated 60 people a year at just one New York City Hospital.

Studies done at the Medical College of Virginia show that THC diminishes the immune system's ability to fight herpes simplex virus and cancer. (2) Doctors have correlated an inability to get rid of genital herpes with THC, because the THC molecule interferes with the particular T-cells (the body's immune cells) which fight the disease. Because THC is immune suppressive, doctors are concerned that use of marijuana may be harmful to AIDS patients whose immune systems are already compromised.

There is 70% more benzopyrene, a known cancer-causing agent, in marijuana than in regular tobacco. Examination of human lung tissue exposed to marijuana smoke over time in a laboratory showed cellular changes called metaplasia, a pre-cancerous condition.

Juvenile crime, unplanned pregnancy, teenage suicides, runaways, depression and psychiatric admissions have all been equated with the rise in popularity of marijuana.

Scientists believe that we still don't know all the long-term damaging effects of marijuana use. *Ongoing studies on brain and genetic damage suggest that marijuana is more harmful than we realize.*

There are 10,500 documented scientific research papers on file at the University of Mississippi on marijuana and not one gives the drug a clean bill of health. The American Medical Association, The National Multiple Sclerosis Society, The American Glaucoma Society, The American Academy of Opthalmology and The American Cancer Society have all rejected marijuana as medicine.

WHAT TO LOOK FOR: Dried stems or seeds, small rolled cigarettes, 1" diameter screen, tiny pipes, cigarette rolling papers, aluminum foil to make pipes, water pipes or bongs, small zip-lock baggies.

SIGNS OF USE: Euphoria, relaxed inhibitions, disoriented behavior, hilarity without cause, time distortion, bloodshot eyes, loss of motivation.

COST: $5.00 to $50.00 per day ($280 per ounce).*

LENGTH OF MARIJUANA HIGH: 4 to 6 hours after smoking.

* **Note:** all prices of drugs listed in the *Problems* section are 'street' or black market prices. Costs vary from place to place and are subject to change.

MARIJUANA

"*The bottom fell out when my addicted 15 year-old dropped out of high school and started living in vacant lots. The only way I knew he was alive was when he called me collect once in a while. I had to prepare mentally for his death.*"
— *Mother of an drug addict*

Other Drugs

Other drugs abused include stimulants, anabolic steroids, inhalants, hallucinogens, narcotics and sedative hypnotics. These drugs are seldom used alone, and it is frequently (but not only) multi-drug use which causes the most lethal reaction. It is to be noted, however, that all drugs are dangerous and have serious side effects.

Many of these are street drugs which can vary radically in strength and purity. Often a youngster has no idea what the strength and purity of a drug might be.

Research has only begun to reveal the extensive damage that drugs cause to the brain, the central nervous system, the heart, the reproductive system, the immune system, in fact the whole body. One of the hazards is overdose/death, which can occur after even one-time use.

Stimulants ('Uppers')

Stimulants are chemicals which speed up the metabolism of cells of the central nervous system. Stimulants such as caffeine, nicotine and cocaine occur naturally in plants. Others, such as amphetamines and diet pills, are synthesized in the laboratory. Laboratory stimulants were developed originally for medical use. Today both natural and synthesized stimulants are widely abused. People abuse them at great risk, because dependency upon them results in permanent damage to the brain and body organs.

Note: Parents sometimes find unfamiliar pills or capsules among their teen's belongings. These pills may be powerful prescription drugs bought on the street. Parents should take them to a pharmacist for indentification.

Cocaine

Cocaine users are up to 62 times more likely to attempt suicide. (1)

Cocaine is a drug which is extracted from the leaves of the coca plant which grows in South America. Like the amphetamines, it stimulates the central nervous system and can cause death by cardiac arrest or respiratory failure. Despite its high cost, this drug has become all too common among adolescents in the suburbs. Cocaine is distributed as a white, odorless, crystalline powder, often adulterated to about half its volume by a variety of other ingredients. Cocaine is usually 'snorted' (inhaled) through the nasal passages. For heightened effect, the drug may be injected into the bloodstream, but this isn't as common as 'snorting'.

Cocaine may also be smoked. Freebase cocaine is cocaine which has been chemically altered to make it smokeable. Freebasing gives a more intense 'high' and also increases the risks associated with using the drug, because smoking is the most direct and rapid way to get the drug to the brain (5-8 seconds).

Appeal — Users feel great, powerful, confident and energetic, as if they can do anything. Cocaine mimics natural adrenal energy and stimulates the pleasure center of the brain.

Harm — Cocaine has the potential for intense psychic dependency. Recurrent users need ever larger doses at shorter intervals to achieve 'highs'. A recent Harvard study reveals that even occasional use can cause permanent brain damage. Brain scans show holes as large as golf balls in the brains of occasional, 'recreational' users. (2) The majority of these holes appear in the frontal lobes which control mood and social behavior.

Cocaine sniffing causes damage to the nasal passages. Perforations, anywhere from the size of a pinhead to the size of a dime, are common among frequent users. Ultimately the inner structure of the nose caves in causing the nose to flatten.

Cocaine craving— The initial rush is extremely intense and pleasurable and users try to recapture the feeling. Sensory 'flashbacks' will trigger the memory, and create a severe desire to use.

"Life revolves around getting 'high.' You use as much as possible as often as possible. You can't be 'normal' when you're off the drug, because you're so depressed." — A recovering cocaine user.

Cocaine crash— After the initial rush of euphoria, the user is often left with a severe depression which can last up to several months. The depression can be as severe as it would be if one suffered a death in the family. Therefore users continue to feed their habit to avoid the crash. Because cocaine destroys the brain's ability to regulate mood and emotions, the cost of a cocaine high is the prolonged inability to experience happiness after the high wears off.

Cocaine overdose — Known as 'caine reaction', an overdose of cocaine can be caused by a fraction of a gram of the drug. Usually it is not fatal, but the user feels like he's going to die. However, when death from overdose does occur, it usually happens during the initial stimulatory phase or during the 'crash,' when respiratory function is depressed and the user goes into a coma. There is also a risk of death in withdrawal from cocaine. Cocaine withdrawal should always be supervisd by a physician.

WHAT TO LOOK FOR: White crystalline powder, small straws, dollar bills rolled up to form straws, small mirrors, razor blades.

SIGNS OF USE: Hyperactivity, followed by depression and excessive sleeping, weight and appetite loss, constant sniffling, nosebleeds.

COST: Cocaine, $100/gram (size of substitute sugar packet). Habit can run as high as $1200 daily).

LENGTH OF COCAINE HIGH: 40 minutes for snorting 2 to 3 'lines' (a 'line' is a narrow strip of cocaine powder, about 3 inches long).

STIMULANTS

Crack Cocaine

Crack cocaine is cocaine mixed with baking soda and water so that a paste is formed. Once the paste is hardened, it can then be broken into pieces which are smoked. Crack is sold in small vials containing 2 to 3 pieces known as 'rocks'. A vial costs only $10 or less, which puts it in easy reach of teens who usually cannot afford the much more expensive pure cocaine.

Appeal — Crack is cheap. Smoking it allows the effects of the drug to reach the brain in a few seconds which gives the user a shorter lasting but extremely intense 'high'.

Harm — Crack creates dependency almost immediately. An overdose of crack cocaine can result in cardiac arrest.

WHAT TO LOOK FOR: Small white or tan crystalline rocks, vials (see-through plastic) with colored caps, miniature zip-lock bags, tiny pipes, soda cans and plastic water bottles with holes in their sides, plastic or glass stems, aluminum with holes in it.

SIGNS OF USE: Loss of appetite, weight loss, mood swings, hyperactivity, insomnia for days followed by crashing for days.

COST: Crack, $10 - $100 per day.

LENGTH Of CRACK HIGH: 20 minutes at most.

Amphetamines

"Before long I could shoot a spoon of speed and still go to school."
— 18 year-old girl

Amphetamines are synthetic drugs which were originally manufactured for medical or scientific applications. By altering the chemical structure of synthetic drugs, black market chemists have created new drugs known as 'designer drugs.' Designer amphetamines, including ice, crank, meth and crystal, were created specifically to be used for drug abuse and to circumvent the law. At first designer drugs were not defined under the law, and therefore black market chemists could not be prosecuted for developing them. Today, however, it is illegal to create designer drugs.

These drugs are extremely dangerous because they are much stronger than organic drugs such as heroin or marijuana, and it is easy to overdose. A second problem is that chemists don't always get the formula right and the end product can be, and in more than a few cases has been, lethal. Finally, because these drugs are untested, the harmful side effects are unknown until they surface in the people who have experimented with the drugs. Other popular designer drugs include MPPP (a heroin substitute, see page 94) and a number of hallucinogens (see page 88).

Amphetamines are a class of synthetic stimulants, known as speed, meth, methamphetamines, crank, crystal, ice and glass. Amphetamines can be taken orally, but shooting, snorting and most recently smoking are the chosen methods among users. Tolerance to amphetamines is quick. A long-term user may need 20 times the initial dose to produce the original 'high'. (1) Users often go on binges, staying up for days at a time, putting severe stress on their bodies.

Appeal — They give the user energy, a feeling of well-being, alertness, self-confidence. Some girls use amphetamines to lose weight.

Harm — The effects of small to moderate doses are increased heartbeat and rate of respiration, increased body temperature and appetite suppression. Prolonged use can cause extreme paranoia which sometimes results in homicidal or suicidal tendencies. Long-term use can also cause hallucinations, sleep deprivation, heart and blood vessel toxicity and severe malnutrition. Death has occurred from overdose.

WHAT TO LOOK FOR: Capsules, pills, white powder, jar of pills of varying colors.

SIGNS OF USE: Insomnia, extreme nervousness, uncomfortable physical sensations ('like bugs crawling on you'), talkativeness, manic energy, increased blood pressure, depression in withdrawal.

COST: $3.00-$5.00 per pill. Teen use might be a few a day.
LENGTH OF AMPHETAMINE HIGH: 4-6 hours for one pill.

STIMULANTS

79

'Ice'

'Ice,' a relatively new designer drug known as glass, batu, shalui, or snot (a reddish liquid methampehtamine base), spread from Hawaii to the east in the summer of 1989. It is more smokeable than crank or crystal meth and therefore more addictive.

Appeal — 'Ice' releases exaggerated feelings of euphoria, alertness, well-being, self-confidence and importance.

Harm — Both cocaine and 'ice' make the user feel capable of doing anything, which is especially dangerous with teenagers who tend to be fearless anyway. Frequent use of 'ice' changes an adolescent's personality. A youngster can hallucinate and ultimately become violent and psychotic.

WHAT TO LOOK FOR: Pipe, glass tubes.

SIGNS OF USE: Extreme insomnia for several days, weight loss, paranoia, aggressive mood swings, severe headaches, heavy sweats.

COST: $5.00-$10.00 a dose.

LENGTH OF ICE HIGH: 6-24 hours.

Diet Pills

The world of fashion has not done us any favor by setting a standard of so-called beauty based on extreme thinness. This has been a factor in adolescent amphetamine use, especially among females. Diet pills include both over-the-counter brands and prescription drugs such as Preludin, Cylert, Bontril, Fastin, Plegine and Tenuatedospan.

Appeal — Weight loss, the ability to surpass fatigue.

Harm — The diet pill known as *speed* is habit forming and dangerous. Users have been known to suffer severe heart palpitations, shortness of breath, insomnia, elevated blood pressure, stomach problems and psychological disturbances. Amphetamines stimulate the central nervous system the way cocaine does.

WHAT TO LOOK FOR: Capsules, pills, white powder, jar of pills of varying colors, over-the-counter diet pill packages.

SIGNS OF USE: Extreme nervousness, loss of weight, long periods of sleep and exhaustion, dilated pupils, talkativeness, insomnia, increased blood pressure, depression in withdrawal.

COST: $5.00 - $7.00 per prescription pill. $6.00 for package of over-the-counter pills which provides pills for 28 days.

LENGTH OF DIET PILL HIGH: 4-6 hours (prescription), 2-4 hours (over the counter).

STIMULANTS

81

"NO ONE ON THIS TEAM USES STEROIDS!"

*"90% of the athletes I know
are on the stuff."*
— *Lyle Alzado, Former NFL Star,* (1)
died May 14, 1992 aged 43.

Anabolic Steroids

Anabolic steroids known as juice, gear and roids are synthesized derivatives of the male hormone testosterone. Steroids have an androgenic or masculinizng effect. They increase such male characteristics as whiskers on the face, lowering of the voice and aggression. These symptoms occur in women who use steroids as well as men. Over 250,000 high school-aged adolescents use steroids to give themselves a competitive edge in sports or in appearance.(2)

Steroids are usually taken in pill form, although they can be injected. Where they are injected, needle sharing occurs which always carries with it the risk of HIV infection. Some users combine or 'stack' steroids in order to maximize their effectiveness. Others take them in cycles, some in pill form and some injectables in order to minimize side effects or to achieve certain effects for particular athletic events.

Since President Bush signed the Anabolic Steroids Control Act in 1990, pushing steroids has been a felony. Nevertheless, the black market moves over $100 million worth of steroids annually. (3) Sales are made in gyms and health clubs, on campuses and through the mail. Steroid addicts claim that they purchase the drugs from trainers, coaches, physicians, pharmacists and pushers at gyms.

Appeal — Increases body size and muscle mass. One can compete at a higher level or look more manly.

Harm — High school athletes in greater and greater numbers are abusing steroids to increase their chances of winning. Some young people start with three little pills a day and work up to nine a day in eight-week cycles. Some teens increase the dosage and forget the cycles. Some 'stack' for quicker results, which means they mix different kinds. And some graduate to injectables.

Steroids can cause severe acne, mood swings and baldness in men. In addition male breasts can grow, kidneys ache and anxiety attacks and insomnia are common. Long-term use can lead to cancerous liver tumors and potentially dangerous plaque buildup in the heart. Even small doses can change the body's chemistry. The

STEROIDS

jawbone, hands, feet, nose, lips and other body parts may grow to grotesque proportions.

Boys as young as thirteen are in some cases paying between $50 and $400 for black market steroids. They don't realize that these drugs may stunt their growth by speeding up bone maturation. They don't know steroids might endanger their still developing reproductive systems, causing shrinking of the testicles as well as impotence. Steroids also affect mental health. Users become aggressive, moody, depressed, irritable, given to 'roid rages'. Girls who use steroids acquire male characteristics and suffer irregular or cessation of menstruation.

Dr. Forest Tennant, Director of Community Health Project Medical Group, says "Lyle Alzado will be the first of many big names to come down with cancer." Widespread steroid use is a relatively new phenomenon, and it will be some time before we understand the long-term harmful effects of the drug. But there is increasing evidence that steroids cause severe damage to internal organs. Long-term use can lead to liver cancer, decreased sex drive and plaque buildup which causes heart disease, and it can permanently stunt growth. Doctors have observed severe depression in long-term users in addition to a tendency toward rages and irrational behavior.

Some physicians have been caught prescribing illegally, but the number who do this is decreasing. Black market steroids are manufactured in underground labs and foreign countries, and many are of questionable quality and purity.

WHAT TO LOOK FOR: Small tablets, liquid vials, injectables.

SIGNS OF USE: Quick weight gain, aggressiveness, rages, unexplained darkening of the skin, persistent breath odor, nosebleeds, acne, doughy breasts.

COST AND LENGTH OF CYCLE: $50-$400 for 6 to 13-week cycle of pills and injectables. $15 will buy a syringe and one cc of testosterone. $95 for Anadrol-50, $40 for 10 ccs of testosterone cypionate, $40 for a bottle of Dianabol.

HGH

When athletes rest their bodies between steroid cycles, they have the option of watching their muscles deflate or doing something other than lifting weights to maintain the bulk. Some adolescents choose to solve this dilemma by taking Human Growth Hormone (HGH), a derivative from the human pituitary gland used to treat children suffering from dwarfism.

HGH is very rare and it is extremely expensive. Unlike steroids, HGH may not deliver even temporary physical 'improvement'. The user may end up with big debts and big risks, but no big muscles. HGH can cause acromegaly, the enlargement of the brow, as well as hands and feet, sometimes called 'Frankenstein's syndrome'. Other side effects can include diabetes or hypertension.

HGH is used frequently in spite of its high cost. 5% of males surveyed are either using HGH or have used it in the past and 31% say that they know someone who uses the drug. A majority of those surveyed were aware of HGH. (1)

WHAT TO LOOK FOR: Vials and injectables.

SIGNS OF USE: Quick and pronounced muscle mass.

COST AND LENGTH: $4000 for a 16-week cycle.

HGH

Inhalants

"We'd buy those cartridges, the ones for whipped cream machines or seltzer bottles. Then we'd puncture them and put the gas in a paper bag or balloon and sniff it."
— *Recovering addict.*

Inhalants are breathable chemicals that produce psychoactive (mind-altering) vapors. People do not usually think of inhalants as drugs because they are not meant to be used as such. They include solvents, aerosols, some anesthetics and other chemicals. Examples are model airplane glue, nail polish remover, lighter and cleaning fluids. Aerosols include paints, hair sprays and other spray products. Young people especially between the ages of 7 and 17 are more likely to abuse inhalants, in part because they are readily available in grocery stores and inexpensive. (1) Kids say they spray the chemical onto their clothing before they go to school, so they can sniff the fumes all day.

Appeal — Temporary stimulation, reduced inhibition, intoxication.

Harm — Deep breathing of the vapors or using a lot over a short period of time may result in losing touch with one's surroundings, a loss of self-control, violent behavior, unconsciousness or even death. Sniffing highly concentrated amounts of solvents or aerosol sprays can produce heart failure and instant death. Inhalants cause death by depressing the central nervous system so much that breathing slows down until it stops. Deliberately inhaling from a paper bag greatly increases the chance of suffocation.

Long-term use can cause weight loss, fatigue and muscle fatigue. Repeated sniffing over a number of years can cause permanent damage to the nervous system; also damage to the liver, kidneys, blood and bone marrow. Use also can cause memory loss and permanent brain damage. Using inhalants while taking other drugs such as alcohol that slow down the body's functions increases the risk of death from overdose.

WHAT TO LOOK FOR: Gas cartridges for whipping cream machines, aerosol spray cans and aerosol paint cans in unusual places, gasoline, paint thinners or glue, cleaning rags, correction fluid and butane gas.

SIGNS OF USE: Hallucinations, dizziness, scrambled words and disconnected sentences. Often the odor of the substance is apparent on the child.

COST: $1.00 to $3.00 for many aerosol products, such as whipped cream, cleaners, glues.

LENGTH OF INHALANT HIGH: From just minutes to an hour.

INHALANTS

Hallucinogens

Hallucinogenic (psychedelic) drugs are both mind-altering and deadly. They are synthetic and they include LSD ('acid'), PCP ('angel dust'), mescaline, and designer variations such as MDMA ('ecstasy'), PMA, TMA, MDA and DMT (called the 'alphabet soup' psychedelics). Users may 'see' sounds and 'hear' colors larger than life, leading the adolescent anywhere from impaired judgment all the way to suicide.

Many psychedelics, particularly LSD, have been called 'mirrors that magnify'. The mood, the emotional state, the insecurities, secrets and worries of the adolescent are highlighted by using hallucinogens, which is particularly dangerous for those teens who are 'unstable'. Some young people have required long-term psychiatric care and hospitalization as a result of 'bad trips'.

Long after the hallucinogens are eliminated from the body the user may find recurrences of the effects of the drug in the form of a fragmentary psychedelic incident such as witnessing the movement of a fixed object. These experiences are called 'flashbacks' and could happen up to two years after use.

Most hallucinogens rapidly produce tolerance or habituation, where the adolescent needs to use higher and higher doses in order to achieve the same 'high'. Tolerance to one hallucinogen produces cross-tolerance to others.

LSD

"I was convinced I knew what everyone was thinking. I thought everyone was out to get me...and then you really start to freak out." — *Teenage LSD user.*

LSD (lysergic acid), the most powerful hallucinogen, is a dangerous mood-altering drug. LSD is usually sold in the form of tablets, thin squares of gelatin (window-panes) or impregnated paper (blotter acid). The average effective oral dose is from 100-250 micrograms, but the amount per dosage varies greatly. The effects of higher doses persist for 10 to 20 hours. Tolerance develops rapidly. LSD is taken orally, licked off paper or colored stamps.

LSD is the fastest growing drug of abuse among the under 20 age group. It has been found not only in high schools and colleges, but in middle schools and even grade schools. LSD arrests have doubled in the past three years. Dr. Lloyd Johnston of the University of Michigan reports that today's adolescents have not seen the consequences experienced in the 60's and 70's, so they don't understand the danger of LSD use. Over 40% of teens say that LSD is easy to obtain and cheap to buy. (1) Marijuana is a major predictor of LSD use. 28% of marijuana users use LSD and 95% of LSD users use marijuana. (2)

Appeal — LSD causes wild sensory illusions and hallucinations, heightened awareness. Users become focused and introverted, and users often take it before listening to music and concerts.

Harm — Physical effects may include dilated pupils, elevated body temperature, increased heart rate and blood pressure, loss of appetite, sleeplessness and tremors. It causes extreme mental disorder often resulting in permanent brain damage. Sensations and feelings may change rapidly. It is common to have a bad psychological reaction to LSD ('bad trip'). The user may experience panic, confusion, suspicion, anxiety and loss of control. LSD use can result in a psychotic reaction which can last months and require hospitalization. Delayed effects or 'flashbacks' can occur months or years after use. LSD trips are marked by bad 'crashes' with feelings of paranoia.

HALLUCINOGENS

89

WHAT TO LOOK FOR: Colored stamps (to lick), small sugar cubes, pills, small brown vials.

SIGNS OF USE: 'Spaced out', severe hallucinations, feelings of detachment, very fatigued, incoherent thoughts and speech, hysteria, elevated body temperature and blood pressure and dilated pupils.

COST: From $10.00 to $25.00 a 'hit'.

LENGTH OF LSD HIGH: 4-8 hours (small dose), 12 hours (medium dose).

Mescaline

Mescaline, known as mesc, buttons or cactus, is the primary active ingredient in the peyote cactus. Usually ground into a powder, peyote is taken orally as a capsule. It can also be produced synthetically.

Appeal — Colorful visions, a mellow LSD-like trip.

Harm — Mescaline, like other hallucinogens, is an extremely dangerous, mind-altering drug which causes extreme mental disorder and often results in permanent brain damage. Its crash is severe and users often take speed to soften the effects.

WHAT TO LOOK FOR: Powder, capsules.

SIGNS OF USE: Confusion, hallucinations.

COST: $5.00 to $10.00 a 'hit'.

LENGTH OF MESC HIGH: 12 hours for an average dose of 7 to 8 buttons.

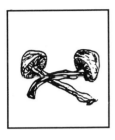

Mushrooms

Like the peyote cactus, psilocybin mushrooms (shrooms) have been used for centuries by some bands of Native Americans in traditional Indian rites. Mushrooms are equivalent to LSD, but organic. Although one hallucinates, it's a more mellow 'high' than LSD. Some teens eat the mushrooms, others boil them and drink the water. To identify the right 'shrooms', the stem is broken in half, and if it turns purple to grey, it is the right mushroom. To preserve the mushrooms before they sell them, dealers keep them freeze-dried in glassine bags.

Appeal — Visions and altered states of consciousness, heightened awareness.

Harm — Mushrooms can cause severe stomach upset, dry heaves, or violent vomiting, and the 'crash' from using mushrooms is severe.

WHAT TO LOOK FOR: Fresh or dried mushrooms.

SIGNS OF USE: Upset stomach, vomiting, 'spaced out'.

COST: Free to users who tramp the countryside to find them. Or $5.00-$10.00.

LENGTH OF MUSHROOM HIGH: 5 to 6 hours. Can vary dramatically with strength.

HALLUCINOGENS

PCP

"I wanted to die. I thought 'God, if You just get me through this one more time, I'll never do it again.' And of course I did." — Recovering Teenager.

PCP, known as angel dust, rocket fuel or crystal, induces bizarre and unexpected effects. The user's behavior becomes unmanageable and there is no way to know what kind of a trip he or she will have. PCP can be bought as a tablet, powder or crystal. It can be a stimulant or a depressant or a hallucinogen. PCP is sometimes mixed with other drugs and the unknowing user panics as the unexpected effects take over. The effects of PCP can vary tremendously, depending on dosage, purity of the drug, the way the drug is taken and the body chemistry of the user. Sometimes marijuana joints or cigarettes are dipped in PCP and then smoked. Or PCP can be eaten with peanut butter, added to fruit juice, injected, snorted, or even absorbed through the skin. Smoking is the most common means of using PCP.

Appeal — The lure of PCP for adolescents is the dangerous adventure it offers. Often users experience a floating sensation along with a physical and emotional numbness. Kids who are going 'wilding' may take PCP first.

Harm — In its liquid form, it is especially dangerous because it's more likely to contain impurities such as cyanide, a poison which is used to carry out death sentences in the gas chamber. Violent episodes, such as falling from great heights or drowning, are not uncommon with PCP. It also produces a mental state similar to schizophrenia which may last anywhere from a few hours to a few days or weeks. There is no known physical addiction to PCP. However, there can be a psychological addiction. When PCP is used frequently, memory, perception, concentration and judgment are all affected, long after the 'high' from the drug has worn off.

WHAT TO LOOK FOR: White powder, tablet, crystal, liquid.

SIGNS OF USE: Slow body movements, decrease in muscular coordination, staggering, 'spaced out', bizarre behavior.

COST: $3.00 per 'bag of dust' (2 marijuana joints laced with PCP).

LENGTH OF PCP HIGH: Low dosage (2-5 mg) - 1 to 2 hours. Medium dosage (10-15 mg) - 6 to 12 hours. Dangerously high dosage (20 mg) - 48 hours.

Ecstasy

Ecstasy, a synthetic, mind-altering drug, also known as Adam, 'XTC' or the hug drug, is especially popular in western and south central areas of the U.S.

Appeal— A party drug, may lead to psychedelic visions, creates warm affectionate feelings, no hangover; the 'high' of cocaine with the sustained effect of LSD. Intoxicating effects last for days.

Harm— Users of ecstasy encounter side effects which include confusion, depression, sleep disorder and paranoia. Its chemical structure is very similar to MDA and methamphetamine which are both known to cause brain damage. Ecstasy has an affinity for the brain cells that regulate movement. Ecstasy kills these cells causing irreversible Parkinson's disease. In some cases, the slowing of movement can reach near immobility much like that seen in the movie 'Awakenings.' A few users have died shortly after taking the drug. Like LSD, ecstasy can cause flashbacks, sometimes weeks after use. Increases in heart rate and blood pressure create a special risk for people with circulatory or heart disease. It has also been to known to affect the fluid in the spinal column.

WHAT TO LOOK FOR: Pills, a little larger than aspirin, can be any color, large sugar-like cubes.

SIGNS OF USE: Confusion, insomnia, paranoia.

COST: $5.00 a 'hit'.

LENGTH OF ECSTASY HIGH: 4 to 6 hours for small dose.

HALLUCINOGENS

93

Narcotics (Opiates)

Narcotics include codeine and morphine, which occur legally in brand-name painkillers, plus the illicit heroin and opium. Opiates, which can be natural or synthetic, act on the central nervous system. Tolerance develops rapidly and physical dependence can result.

Heroin

Heroin (junk, horse, smack) accounts for 90% of opiate abuse in the United States. Pure heroin is a white powder with a bitter taste. Illicit heroin may vary in color from white to dark brown because of impurities. Street heroin is rarely pure, but is usually diluted with sugars, starch or powdered milk. As a powder heroin is inhaled through nasal passages, smoked or injected. To inject the drug, it is heated in a spoon and reduced to a liquid and injected into the blood stream. MPPP or White China is a synthetic heroin-like drug. Bad batches of black market MPPP have been known to cause paralysis and, in some cases, death.

In 1993, therapists report that more heroin addicts are now smoking rather than injecting heroin because of the HIV scare. They also report that cocaine addicts are switching to heroin because a heroin addict lives much longer than a cocaine addict. Growers are producing more heroin and less cocaine for the same reason.

Appeal — Heroin is a depressant with intoxicating effects. Produces a feeling of euphoria.

Harm — Heroin impedes the user's ability to reason. Its synthetic form, known as a 'designer drug', has proven to be even more deadly and addictive. Initial euphoria is often followed by drowsiness, nausea and vomiting. An overdose may produce slow and shallow breathing, clammy skin, convulsions, coma and possibly death. Tolerance to heroin develops rapidly and dependence is likely. The use of contaminated syringes may result in AIDS and hepatitis. When a heroin-dependent person stops taking the drug, withdrawal begins within 4-6 hours after the last injection. Full-blown withdrawal symptoms include shaking, sweating, vomiting, a runny nose and eyes, muscle cramps and chills. Many people compare these symptoms to severe influenza.

WHAT TO LOOK FOR: Burnt bottle caps, tiny glassine bags with decals (markings show user where drugs came from), syringes, eye droppers, spoons for heating and dissolving powders, cords and belts for tourniquets, blood stain on shirt sleeve, cotton balls stained with blood.

SIGNS OF USE: Needle marks on arms and back of knees, watery eyes, 'nodding', too relaxed or very agitated, inability to handle simple problems.

COST: $40 - $200 per day.

LENGTH OF HEROIN HIGH: 2 to 4 hours.

NARCOTICS

Codeine

Codeine is a natural by-product of morphine, although it produces less respiratory depression and sedation. Codeine is often prescribed for the relief of pain in the form of pure codeine tablets; or it can be combined with other aspirin and painkilling products.

Appeal — Kills pain, relaxes.

Harm — Codeine is a strong narcotic found in prescription cough medicines often left in the medicine cabinet, which makes it easily accessible to children. Codeine is addictive and can lead to stronger drugs.

WHAT TO LOOK FOR: Unexpected disappearance of cough medicine or pills.

SIGNS OF USE: Drunkenness, staggering, slurring.

COST: $40+ per pint for prescription cough medicine.

LENGTH OF CODEINE HIGH: 2 to 4 hours.

Sedatives/Hypnotics ('Downers')

Sedatives/hypnotics were developed to treat nervousness and insomnia by depressing the central nervous system. Barbiturates are the most common sedatives and, as with alcohol, people can become physically addicted. Barbiturates include Methaqualone, Seconal, Valium, Xanax (tranquilizers) and Dalmane (sleeping pills), available by prescription. Under a doctor's care these drugs can be useful and harmless. But all too often they are abused by adolescents buying them illegally on the street or by persons who exceed the prescription. Abusers suffer withdrawal symptoms as severe as those associated with heroin withdrawal.

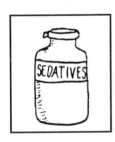

Valium

Valium (Vals) was developed in the 1950's and accounted for more than half of the sedatives/hypnotics sold by the 1970's. (1) The effect of a sedative/hypnotic is similar to that of alcohol.

Appeal — Users feel relaxed, comfortable.

Harm — The most serious problem caused by Valium is addiction. Withdrawal from Valium should always be done under a physician's care, because addiction is so severe that more people have died from Valium withdrawal than from Valium overdose. Withdrawal symptoms occur 24 to 72 hours after taking the drug because the effect of the drug is long-lasting. Withdrawal symptoms include craving for the drug, anxiety, sleep disturbances and even hallucinations. These symptoms continue for days and peak in one to three weeks. People have experienced convulsions in Valium withdrawal and 80-90% of Valium abusers suffer severe withdrawal.(1) The combination of Valium and alcohol can cause death by overdose.

WHAT TO LOOK FOR: Small white tablets.

SIGNS OF USE: Overly relaxed state, excessive sleepiness.

COST: $5.00 per pill.

LENGTH OF VALIUM HIGH: 24 to 72 hours.

Methaqualone

Thought to be effective as an aphrodisiac and also mistakenly believed to be non-addicting, methaqualone is a synthetic barbiturate widely abused by many adolescents. It has been marketed in the United States under various brand names such as Quaalude, Parest, Optimil, Somnafac and Sapok.

Appeal— Creates relaxed, numb state, overall sedation, mild euphoria, suppresses inhibitions, aphrodisiac.

Harm— The drug is taken orally in tablet form, and in large doses can cause coma accompanied by thrashing movements or convulsion. Continued usage leads to tolerance and dependence.

WHAT TO LOOK FOR: Tablets.

SIGNS OF USE: Slow movement, 'spaced out' behavior.

COST: $5-$10 each tablet.

LENGTH OF METHAQUALONE HIGH: 4 to 6 hours.

Multi-Drug Use

Teens who are looking for a better 'high' frequently use two or more drugs either in combination or sequentially. The two drugs most commonly combined are alcohol and marijuana. Most teens using marijuana also drink alcohol.(1) A high intake of alcohol depresses the drinker's breathing center, causing breathing to stop. At this level of drinking the vomiting center of the brain is usually activated, thereby saving the lives of many teenagers who overdose on alcohol. When alcohol and marijuana are combined, however, marijuana suppresses the brain's vomiting center leading to greater risk of death.

Most adolescent cocaine users take other drugs to counteract the unpleasant side effects of cocaine. 92% use marijuana, 85% use alcohol. (2) Some are using heroin to counteract 'cocaine crash'. The mix of cocaine and alcohol creates a third chemical (cocaethylene) that intensifies cocaine's euphoric effects while possibly increasing the risk of sudden death. According to the University of Miami School of Medicine, cocaethylene worsens the cocaine craving and possibly causes addictions that are harder to break. Users with significant coronary disease who mix alcohol and cocaine run 21.5 times the risk of sudden death than do users of cocaine alone, according to the National Institute on Drug Abuse.(3) *Multi-drug use is a dangerous gamble which all too frequently ends in death.*

As the teen adds additional drugs to the combination, the risks multiply. Each drug added brings medical, psychological and emotional reactions which can be unpredictable. The majority of young people ending up in treatment centers have multi-drug problems.

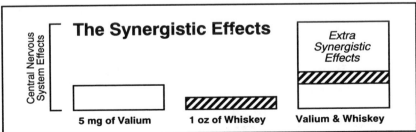

When alcohol and a sedative are combined, a chemical reaction occurs which is stronger than the sum of the two drugs. (4)

"I can quit any time," is the motto of the addict.
It is equally common for the family
of the abuser to ignore the problem,
thus enabling the addict to continue abusing.

Addiction

"My son was a three-letter varsity man, voted MVP, a leader, a good student...and a drug addict."

Denial is a natural manifestation of addiction. A substance abuser denies any problem to protect his/her use of the substance upon which he/she has become dependent. "I can quit any time," is the motto of the addict. It is equally common for the family of the abuser to ignore the problem, thus enabling the addict to continue abusing.

What Is Addiction?

Most experts agree that addiction, whether it be to alcohol or drugs, is a compulsion to use a chemical substance despite negative consequences. There is disagreement, however, about the various causes of addiction and how much addiction is environmental and how much genetic. *The following causes are suspected of contributing to addiction:*

1. **Disease Theory.** This theory is based on the idea that alcoholism and drug addiction result from inherited genetic deficiencies. There are people who are more susceptible to addiction than others. They metabolize alcohol differently and they have a lower level of certain brain hormones than people who are less susceptible. AA (Alcoholics Anonymous) subscribes to this thought and teaches its members that an addict who has stopped using is 'in recovery' for the remainder of his/her life and should not try to become a social user.

2. **Environment.** Some people are more susceptible due to their life circumstances. Peer pressure, media hype and stress cause people to seek alcohol or drugs. If using makes them feel better, they do it again, and in time the stages of chemical dependency run their course.

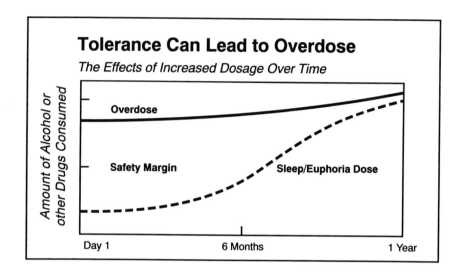

Tolerance Can Lead to Overdose

The Effects of Increased Dosage Over Time

Amount of Alcohol or other Drugs Consumed

Overdose

Safety Margin

Sleep/Euphoria Dose

Day 1   6 Months   1 Year

"It only took me one or two 'hits' (puffs) to get 'high' when I started using drugs, but now it takes me a lot to get stoned." — A high school junior.

---

3. **Changes in the Body Chemistry of the User.**

   - *Tissue dependence.* Changes in body cell chemistry cause the user to 'need' the drug to avoid adverse reactions such as convulsions (physical addiction).

   - *Psychic dependence.* Drugs alter the mood or the state of mind of the user in a way which is pleasurable and which he/ she habitually tries to reproduce (psychological addiction).

   - *Tolerance.* Tolerance occurs when larger and larger doses of a drug are needed to achieve a 'high'. *As the user increases the amount of the drug, he or she moves closer and closer to the overdose level and, unfortunately, some ultimately reach it and die.* It should be noted that inverse tolerance occurs occasionally and causes a user to suddenly have an intense reaction to a drug which had stopped 'working'.

102

Not My Child... Take a Second Look

Parents often miss clues that their children are using alcohol or other drugs. Sometimes this is because they don't recognize the clues; sometimes it's because they don't want to recognize them. Parents must keep an open mind about the possibility of their child drinking or using drugs - and be vigilant.

"I know other kids are taking drugs, but I can't believe mine would."

Most parents accept the fact that drugs are a problem of epidemic proportions but they prefer to believe that it is somebody else's child who has the problem, not their own. This kind of denial is very dangerous. Your best defense against drug abuse is to realize that no family is immune to the problem. It can and does occur in all types of families.

"My child is an honor student and captain of the tennis team. I'm not worried about her."

Parents often feel that if their children are good students who have goals and interests, they are not going to get involved in alcohol and other drugs. Unfortunately statistics show that all kinds of kids - honor students, athletes, class presidents - can have drug problems. Just because your adolescent doesn't fit the stereotype doesn't mean that drugs are not being used.

"Surely you wouldn't expect me to search my child's belongings?"

While an adolescent is entitled to some privacy, you are entitled to know what is going on in your house. Alcohol and other drug users get 'high' in their bedrooms and stash their drug paraphernalia there. Not wanting to find drug clues in our kids' bedrooms is part of our denial system. No parent wants to face these facts, but it sometimes is necessary to look.

ADDICTION

"I wouldn't recognize drugs or drug paraphernalia if I fell over them."

Most parents do not know what drugs look like, or what clues to look for. This information is essential, especially since some of the clues are ordinary household items such as aluminum foil, which kids use to make pipes. Local police departments have brochures on drug paraphernalia, and many have it on display for parents to come and see.

"My child seems different, and his grades have dropped. He's hanging around with a different crowd."

Investigate immediately if your teenager suddenly seems very 'different', especially if his basic values change, his friends change, phone calls change character, grades are slipping, interest in favorite sports or hobbies decline or if he seems depressed. Having a blood test done may help.

"My child experimented and assured me that he wasn't going to use marijuana again."

An adolescent who admits to using alcohol and other drugs once may be using them on a regular basis. The admission is a way of minimizing his involvement - to you and to himself. Again, it's important to investigate further to learn the real truth.

"Recently I've noticed money missing from my wallet."

If valuables or money are missing, do not ignore this danger signal. Some drugs are expensive. Once the dependency has escalated and adolescents have started buying their own drugs, they need additional money. It's hard to believe, but they may resort to stealing money, silver or anything that can be sold for cash.

"I experimented when I was a teen and I outgrew it."

Do not deceive yourself. Times are different. Drugs are stronger, drugs are an epidemic and alcohol and other drug use is dangerous. Do not lose your perspective on what is considered to be normal adolescent behavior.

104

"Yes, my 17 year-old son takes steroids in order to compete more favorably on the playing field. But he tells me he can stop any time he wants to."

Although steroids aren't physically addictive, it's hard to stop once you've started. Some adolescents say they'll take steroids until they like their performance or physique and then they'll quit. Bulging biceps and ham-hock thighs quickly collapse without continuing steroid use. So do the accompanying feelings of being on top of the world. Often people who stop start up again. (See page 83, Anabolic Steroids.)

"I've found cans of spray paint in my 13 year-old daughter's room. I've heard of inhalants, but surely a 13 year-old girl wouldn't do that."

According to a University of Michigan Institute for Social Research study, high school seniors say they first tried inhalants during the seventh or eighth grade. (See page 86, Inhalants.)

"My son is only 13 years old. I don't have to worry about substance abuse for another couple of years."

The percentage of students using drugs by the sixth grade has tripled over the past decade. In the early 1960's marijuana use was virtually non-existent among 13 year-olds, but all recent major surveys reveal significant use among middle schoolers.

"My 16 year-old daughter told me she only smoked one marijuana joint. That seemed pretty innocent. I wasn't overly concerned. In the sixties I used to smoke marijuana once in a while."

The drugs students are taking today are more potent, more dangerous and more addictive than ever. The marijuana produced today is five to twenty times stronger than that available as recently as 10 years ago. (See page 70, Marijuana.)

ADDICTION

"My daughter spends time at her friend's house when no adults are at home. Recently when she and her friend were alone, they invited boys over. When I complained to the friend's mother, she told me to mind my own business. What should I do?"

As a parent your primary responsibility is to protect your child. Adolescents should not be left alone on a regular basis. Even though your neighbor does not sound very cooperative you need to inform her that your daughter is not allowed at her house when there is no one at home. Make sure your daughter understands the consequences if she decides to disobey your rules.

"After his high school graduation, my son is invited to a keg party which is being hosted by other class parents. The parents believe that by throwing a keg party at their home they can control drinking and driving. I don't want to seem overprotective, but I would rather my son went to a dry party."

It's O.K. to be protective. Call the parents who are buying the keg and remind them that it's illegal to buy alcohol for children under 21. Furthermore, there are serious legal ramifications if one of the children gets hurt. Someone may appear to be able to drive who really isn't. Someone may get toxic with alcohol or an intoxicated youth may have a non-driving accident.

"My 13 year-old has been going to the mall after school with her friends. I've heard that teens push drugs at malls, but I don't believe that my child's friends would get involved in that."

Malls can provide an arena for unwholesome activites. Young people who loiter in malls at best are not doing anything worthwhile. At worst, they may be getting into serious trouble. Be vigilant about your children's activities and about their friends. Get to know their friend's parents and work with them to establish common rules for all your children. Work with the schools, the Y's or the Scouts to provide supervised after-school activities for your children.

"There are people in our town who go away for the weekend and leave their teenagers home alone. Teens left alone throw all-night parties which I know my children attend. I don't approve of this, but I don't know what to do."

You need to set strict rules for your children so that you always know where they are. There are uncaring people in nearly every town who leave their homes and children unsupervised. What you and your friends can do is investigate Safe Homes, a nationwide program which discourages this kind of behavior. Families sign up and commit to never leaving their homes unsupervised. You may want to write to the families in question and get like-minded parents to write as well.

"If you discover that your child is abusing alcohol or other drugs, there are adolescent counseling and treatment programs throughout your state. Turn to page 121 to find help."

ADDICTION

Warning Signs of Adolescent Substance Abuse and Other Emotional Problems

Certain behavior can warn you that your child may be involved with drugs. Even though the norms for adolescent behavior can be broad, there are various warning signals. Trust your instincts. Don't ignore odd behavior. If you suspect trouble, seek professional help (see page 121). Here is a checklist of signs and symptoms that something may be wrong:

☐ **Abrupt changes in mood or attitude** — virtually all mood-altering drugs produce mood swings from euphoria to depression. An adolescent may be passive one minute and hostile the next.

☐ **Personality changes** — a normally energetic and outgoing young person becomes chronically depressed and uncommunicative.

☐ **Defensiveness** — blaming others or claiming to be persecuted or victimized.

☐ **Overly emotional** — inappropriately happy, depressed, hostile or angry.

☐ **Overly self-centered** — adolescents who always have to have their own way and will do anything to have it.

☐ **Tendency to manipulate** — making excuses for failure. Finding ways to have other people handle their responsibilities or deal with their problems or the consequences of their actions.

☐ **Strained communication** — unwillingness or inability to discuss important issues or concerns.

☐ **Withdrawal from family activities** — refusing to eat at family meals, participate in celebrations or holidays or make any adjustments to family life.

☐ **Change in dress and friends** — wearing clothes, jewelry and hair styles imitating drug culture standards. Spending time with suspicious friends who refuse to meet parents, look them in the eye or talk to them.

108

☐ **Lack of self-discipline** — inability to follow rules, complete household chores or school assignments, keep appointments.

☐ **Apathy** — little or no interest in meaningful activities like clubs, hobbies, sports or other extra-curricular activities.

☐ **School problems** — excessive tardiness, absences, drop in grades, failure to turn in assignments and take tests, suspensions or expulsions.

☐ **Anxious behavior** — chronically jittery, jerky, uneven movements, fearfulness, compulsiveness and talkativeness.

☐ **Excess sleeping** — or sleeping at unusual times. Drugs leave teens tired.

Children who fit into any of the following categories may be at especially high risk of alcohol or other drug abuse:

☐ Child who suffers from emotional stress resulting from trouble in the home, problems at school, breakup with a boyfriend/girlfriend, lack of popularity or sports achievement, or concern over the future.

☐ Child who is rebellious. Rebellion is manifested in refusing to accept authority, ignoring rules or breaking the law.

☐ Child who is anxious because he cannot please perfectionist parents or achieve his own expectations.

☐ Child who suffers from low self-esteem and doesn't like himself.

☐ Child who is suggestible and runs with peers who use.

☐ Child whose family or community condone drinking/drug use.

☐ Child who has a genetic predispostion. Are there alcohol or other drug addicts in the family?

ADDICTION

Stages of Chemical Dependency

Substance use almost always begins before the age of 20. The absence of serious physical consequences in the early stages can confirm the user's belief that the chemical is safe and controllable. *Chemical use is often described as having four stages of progression:* curiosity and experimentation, learning the mood swing, seeking the mood swing (planned use) and complete dependence (burnout). With teenagers who progress to addiction, complete dependence can occur anywhere from six months to several years after stage one begins. *In the teen years, the ideal use is no use.*

Stages One and Two are invisible: the warning signs are not yet obvious.

Curiosity and Experimentation

 Motivated by peer pressure and curiosity, a Stage One teenager indulges only occasionally but does not purchase his own substances. Though alcohol and other drugs play no significant role in his life, he learns that moods can be elevated through chemicals. No behavioral changes are evident yet.

Learning the Mood Swing

 A Stage Two adolescent gets intoxicated more frequently, usually at week-end gatherings or during school holidays and summer vacations. His use is not premeditated and he does not go out of his way to find substances. The user learns that the chemical makes one feel good. Few unpleasant effects occur. The chemicals most frequently involved are tobacco, inhalants, alcohol and/ or marijuana. Small amounts produce a 'high' because no tolerance has built up. At this stage parents are usually unaware of any usage.

In Stages Three and Four the warning signs are obvious.

Seeking the Mood Swing

3 This stage is considered drug abuse as opposed to drug use. If your child reaches this stage, you can't deal with the problem by yourself. Professional intervention is essential. The key difference is that the Stage Three teenager actively seeks to alter his mood, believing comfort and pleasure can be derived only through chemicals. His emotions swing between extreme highs and lows, with no middle ground. He gets stoned by himself, including during the week, and goes out of his way to procure substances. Grooming and schoolwork decline, friendships change, family relationships sour as he becomes secretive and alienated. He becomes careless about his habit, perhaps forgetting to conceal substances and paraphernalia. He vehemently denies having a problem. Vandalism, shoplifting, stealing, lying and/or sexual promiscuity are common. As drug use and tolerance increase, stealing from parents and siblings may begin in order to pay for drugs. At this stage, you will notice many of the warning signs listed on pages 108 and 109.

Complete Dependence

4 A Stage Four adolescent's condition deteriorates drastically. He is now psychologically and/or physically dependent on substances and desperately needs higher doses just to feel 'normal'. The bulk of his time is spent getting hold of and using drugs, and he cannot kick his addiction without professional treatment. Friends are exclusively other users, and home life becomes a shambles. A Stage Four abuser has usually failed or dropped out of school, cannot hold a job, 'steals or deals,' and is beset by guilt and feelings of worthlessness. He may suffer from blackouts, impaired memory, flashbacks, frequent illness or suicidal thoughts. Life centers on getting 'high'. The child may advance to hallucinogens, cocaine or crack. Drug use becomes a necessity, not a choice. Attempts to reduce dosage or stop usage fail. The adolescent has a 'druggie look' and there are many physical changes. At least one of the parents is often still in denial. Marital relationships tend to become strained. As this stage progresses the teenager may become known by the police. Health deteriorates. Parents may separate, give up or turn the child out of the house. **Death is not uncommon.**

ADDICTION

111

Related Teen Problems

Substance abuse is only one problem afflicting today's young people. Some develop eating disorders, some suffer severe depression, some get involved in crime and some engage in promiscuous behavior. Each one of these problems is often tied to substance abuse, but can occur independently. If your child appears to meet the description of someone with *any* of the following disorders, *get help immediately.* A list of places to find help appears on pages 125 and 154.

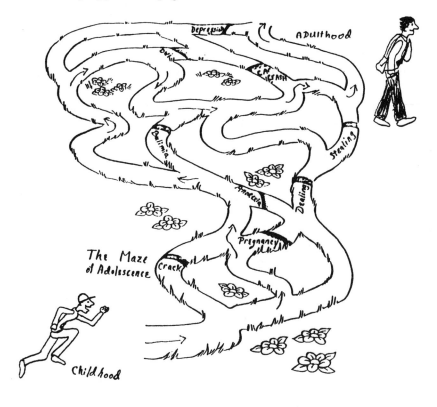

Substance abuse is only one problem afflicting today's young people.

Eating Disorders

Eating disorders mostly affect women in our society. They are characterized by an obsession with food, fat, weight loss and exercise. The friends of adolescents often recognize the problem first and, if they express a concern to an adult, it should be passed along to the afflicted girl's parents immediately.

Bulimia

Bulimia is an illness in which a person binges (overeats and feels out of control) but so fears weight gain that she 'purges' - sometimes by vomiting or fasting or exercising or abusing laxatives.

Signs of Bulimia— preoccupation with weight and obsession with food, weight swings, food disappearing, depression, cessation of periods, possession of laxatives, swollen cheeks due to parotid gland dysfunction.

Anorexia

Anorexia is an illness in which a person feels driven to lose weight and feels fat even as she continues to lose weight through self-starvation.

Signs of Anorexia — weight loss, increasing concern with food and weight (feeling 'fat' though she's thin), cessation of menstrual periods, compulsive exercise.

"You always hear the guys talking about the girls who lost weight. They go after the pretty, skinny girls." — Anorexic teenage girl.

Teenage Sexual Activity

Teenagers fall in love. They always have. Consider Romeo and Juliet. In today's world many of them act on their feelings and get sexually involved. Opinions vary greatly about how the subject should be handled by schools, by the entertainment industry and the media and by parents themselves. However you handle the subject, you need to understand the extent of sexual activity among teenagers.

1994 Statistics Reveal that

- 73% of all teenage boys have intercourse before age 18. (1)
- 56% of all teenage girls have intercourse before age 18. (1)
- 1,040,000 teenage girls become pregnant each year. (1)
- One third of all sexually active teens used <u>no</u> contraception the first time they had sex. (1)
- Four in ten teenage pregnancies end in abortion. (1)
- In a study done in the 1980's, 83% of a group of adolescents surveyed said the best age for intercourse was a later one than the one at which they began having sex. (3)
- One out of four (3,000,000) sexually active teenagers contracts a sexually transmitted disease before graduating from high school. (2)
- AIDS, herpes simplex, chlamydia, gonorrhea and syphilis have all been transmitted by sexually active teenagers. (2)
- Nearly one in four teenagers who experience a premarital pregnancy becomes pregnant again within two years. (1)
- The fastest growing segment of the HIV-infected population is made up of people who are less than 25 years old, many of whom became infected in their teens. (2)

Suicidal Feelings

Teenage suicide is often associated with substance use and abuse. Someone who is depressed or in crisis is more likely to attempt or complete suicide under the influence of alcohol or drugs. Conversely, drug or alcohol use can result in depression and stress from which suicidal urges can emerge. Unhappiness from a failed sexual relationship can also be a catalyst for a suicide attempt. Adolescent suicide rates have tripled in the last 20 years, and drugs are a leading cause. Adolescents may see suicide as a solution to problems and are likely to be impulsive in their suicidal behavior. Suicide is now the third leading cause of death in young people (accidents are #1 and homicide #2). Alcohol and other drugs are a leading contributor in forming the idea of suicide, attempting it and/or completing it. About 5000 youths commit suicide each year and roughly 500,000 attempt it. (1)

Your teenager may be suffering from severe *depression* IF

☐ He threatens to harm himself.

☐ He can't cope even with simple tasks.

☐ He's chemically addicted.

☐ He's violent.

☐ He's dangerously reckless.

☐ His behavior becomes bizarre.

☐ He has been physically or sexually abused.

Your child may be *at risk* for suicide IF

- ☐ He has suffered sexual abuse.

- ☐ He is an alcohol or other drug abuser.

- ☐ He lives with unresolved family conflict.

- ☐ He is depressed.

Your teenager may be *contemplating* suicide IF

- ☐ He has expressed verbally or in writing a wish to die.

- ☐ You uncover a specific suicide plan.

- ☐ You find what appears to be a will.

- ☐ He gives away prized possessions to friends.

- ☐ He seems hopeless and unable to see viable options.

- ☐ He has become withdrawn from family and friends.

- ☐ His grades have dropped and he cuts classes frequently.

- ☐ He experiences a large weight gain or loss.

- ☐ He is self-destructive.

IF YOU EVEN SUSPECT YOUR CHILD IS SUICIDAL, CALL 911 AND GET HELP IMMEDIATELY.

(See page 125 and 154 for an idea of available counseling and treatment resources.)

Drug Dealing and Crime

Drug dealers often recruit youngsters between 8 and 12 years of age to be spotters, lookouts and sellers. (1)

Teen Drug Dealing

In the adolescent community almost anyone could be a drug dealer. The dealer could be selling to his or her circle of friends or to many people. In some cases, teens give drugs to friends or trade them for goods or services. Often teens are trained to distribute for people who work out of a local shop or van. Teens often sell at malls using beepers to stay in touch with distributors and regular customers. Some sell drugs to pay for their own habits. Others sell but don't use.

Drugs which enter the youth market are exchanged two to five times between the initial purchase from the adult to the final sale in school of 'nickel' ($5.00) or 'dime' ($10.00) bags. The teen making the purchase from the adult is the 'dealer'. Adolescents buying from him or from another adolescent who already bought from the 'dealer' are called 'sellers'. The young dealer is part of the adolescent community, and is at the same time a business person in the world of drugs. Typically, this child knows current prices and quantities and can quickly calculate profits.

Although most drug dealing originates in the cities, suburbanites find drugs easy to obtain. Young suburban adults purchase from city dealers and return to their towns to sell through a network which includes adolescents. One Connecticut city has set up a maze of concrete street dividers in its most drug-infested neighborhood to make it difficult for out-of-towners to reach drug dealers from the interstate.

Gangs

The previous page describes how drug dealers use children to distribute drugs. In many cities in America today, gangs of adolescents and pre-adolescents have formed to serve the drug trade. Therefore any town or city which experiences significant drug use has the potential to become a home for a gang.

Though not always the case, gangs tend to be ethnically exclusive. There are white Skinheads, black Crips and Pirus, Filipino Pinoi gangs, Samoan Crips, Chinese Tongs, Korean Killers, Hispanic Locos, among others. Chapters of a particular gang can exist in many cities throughout the country, creating a network through which drugs can be marketed. Members of a gang in one state may contact members of the same gang in another state to form a drug connection.

Each gang has its own identifying characteristics. Skinheads, for example, like to wear leather jackets and combat boots, the Crips like to wear blue, and some gangs require tattoos. Gangs have their own peculiar hand signs used to signal other members of the gang.

A gang will identify with certain rock groups and play that group's music more than others. The rock groups chosen are usually those whose music is explicitly violent or glorifies Satanism. Specific graffiti identify specific gangs and members draw their symbols on buildings to define their territory or offend other gangs by drawing them outside their own territory. Gang fighting breaks out when one gang encroaches on another's territory to gain supremacy over areas where the drug trade is most lucrative.

The appeal of gang life is very seductive to a youth who feels shut out of the mainstream. It offers him a way to belong to something he deems important. Gangs have a strict hierarchy and there are many rules which offer structure to a child whose life has been without discipline. In a warped way, it fills a need where home life has lacked social order.

Drug Related Crime

Drug dependency often leads to crime, because addicts resort to both property crime and crimes of violence in order to support a drug habit. Furthermore, many crimes are committed simply because alcohol and other drugs lower inhibitions against behaving violently.

1992 statistics reveal:

- Drug use among inmates is as high as 282% greater than use in the general population.
- About 30% of inmates used *one or more drugs every day* before incarceration.
- Marijuana was the drug of choice by far of low security prisoners and heroin the drug of choice by far among high security prisoners.
- In 65% of all homicides, the perpetrators, the victims or both had been drinking alcohol.

Alcohol and drug-related homicides are increasing dramatically across the nation and some murderers admit their drug use in order to exploit it as a defense. Drug cases choke our justice system. Some judges report that they cannot attend to other criminal matters as a result of dealing with drug-related crime. More than half of all murder arrestees are under the age of 25, and the majority are alcohol and drug abusers. (2) In New York City, 92% of those arrested for robbery tested positive for drugs. (3)

Drugs not only lead to crime, they contribute to multiple offenses. *Research in Brief,* published by the U.S. Department of Justice, reports that 51% of youths arrested tested positive for cocaine and that they committed four times as many crimes as youths who tested negative. (4)

Professionals feel that by identifying addicts while they are young and effectively rehabilitating them, we can simultaneously reduce addiction and crime.

Arrested Development

Alcohol and drug use damage the adolescent much faster than the adult. Anything, good or bad, that goes into the adolescent body is assimilated in the system faster. A teenager can become addicted five times more quickly than an adult.

Developing systems can be held back or damaged by alcohol and drugs. Drugs stunt or delay sexual and physical development and they can impair a child's immune system. Ethical, moral and emotional maturation can also be impaired because drugs and alcohol depress the parts of the developing brain that control social behavior. If alcohol or drug use continues through adolescence into adulthood, some social skills are never learned.

Studies show that when a child is using chemicals, he/she doesn't learn social amenities from the trial/error system because errors just don't register. The teen therefore just doesn't learn the lesson. It is important for parents to understand that their drug-dependent child's development may have been arrested. A 17 year-old, therefore, who has used drugs continuously since 13 can have the emotional make-up of a 13 year-old.

Help for Parents

When you seek counseling, caring people respond
and let you know you are not alone.

Discovery

Nothing is more frightening, upsetting or confusing than to discover that your child *might* be abusing alcohol or other drugs. Remember alcohol is a drug. If your child is drinking regularly, he or she may have an addiction. And such an addiction is just as serious as an addiction to an illicit drug.

Frequently parents do not see the actual abuse. Rather, they see signs that make them suspicious. Their child's friends change, his or her dress changes, or he or she loses interest in a favorite sport. Sometimes parents find actual evidence, like roll papers, pipes or hidden alcohol. Most parents, particularly if their child is in early adolescence, find it easy to deny even clear signs of abuse.

A wise parent will accept that there may be a problem. At the very least, parents should consult the school nurse or counselor, a favorite teacher or clergy. People who see a child outside the home may see the child differently. They may put a parent's mind at ease or they may concur that there is an abuse problem. *No concern should go uninvestigated.*

If the worst appears to be true, parents need to keep cool. Panic is the enemy. The first step is to express both love and concern to the child. The second is to convince the child to talk to a substance abuse counselor. An experienced professional will be able to diagnose the problem and recommend proper treatment.

Without the help of a professional, most parents are unable to gauge the seriousness of their child's substance abuse. Addictions in children are usually a sign of other unresolved problems. It is essential to discover whether a child has been abusing alcohol or other drugs for a short time or is seriously addicted — and why. *The longer an addiction goes untreated, the harder it is to cure — especially in adolescents.*

123

This section addresses parents' concerns about how and where to get professional help for a troubled teen. It lists sources to turn to for help and describes the many treatment options. It also explains the role of the family in recovery and includes information on family support groups. At the end of the section there is a discussion of legal obligations and penalties for alcohol and drug violations.

How to Seek Professional Help

A number of sources can guide you to a treatment professional. Any one of the following ought to be able to help you find a counselor who specializes in adolescent treatment.

1.   Each state has a *mental health/substance abuse commission.* Each commission should have an updated list of state-financed substance abuse professionals and clinics. Call the commission in your state and ask for the telephone number of a professional in your area. Your local library will have a list of your state agencies.

2.   Today, many *hospitals* have alcohol and other drug treatment professionals on staff, as well as detox units or rehabilitation centers. Very likely your local hospital can steer you to help.

3.   Most *schools* have a resident psychologist or social worker who frequently works with local professionals, especially those who specialize in adolescent problems.

4.   Most *churches and synagogues* have clergy trained in family counseling. You may want to turn to your minister, priest or rabbi.

5.   *The Yellow Pages* list local treatment professionals, often under the heading "Alcoholism and Substance Abuse Treatment."

What to Discuss with the Professional

Once parents find help, there are many questions to discuss with their professional about addiction, cost, the treatment process and about how to handle things at home. This section addresses each of these issues. You should feel free to discuss any of them with your professional.

What is Abuse?

Abuse occurs when a *legal* drug is taken for a purpose other than the one for which it was prescribed. Abuse also occurs when alcohol is used to excess or an *illegal* drug is taken which can harm the user. When experimentation progresses to compulsive use, abuse and dependency result. (See Stages of Chemical Dependency, page 110).

What is Addiction?

Addiction is the compulsive use of a substance resulting in physical or psychological dependency usually accompanied by increased tolerance. An addicted person cannot resist using and loses control over the intake of the drug.

What is Denial?

Denial is the protection which allows one to assimilate devastating information slowly and somewhat eases the shock. Both the substance abuser and his family are usually in denial, and both have a tendency to underplay or minimize the addiction and its consequences. As a result denial all too often keeps the abuser out of treatment.

What is Alcoholism?

1. *Loss of Control* — an alcoholic cannot stop drinking when he/she ought to.

2. *Progression* — an alcoholic gradually becomes obsessed with drinking. He/she drinks more often and, in time, alcohol becomes the main focus of life. This is also true of other drugs.

3. *Withdrawal* — symptoms include headaches, nausea, vomiting and the 'shakes' when the individual stops drinking. Withdrawal symptoms vary with each kind of drug dependency.

4. *Personality Change* — there is a noticeable Jekyll and Hyde transformation with alcoholics. When drunk, the alcoholic behaves differently.

5. *Blackouts* — the alcoholic experiences a kind of amnesia and doesn't remember what happened when he was drinking, even though he appears to be conscious. A blackout can last a few minutes or entire days.

How Do I Know If My Child is Addicted?

It is sometimes hard for parents to tell. However, if you believe that a substance has become the focus of your child's life, you should get a diagnosis from a treatment professional and discuss drug testing.

How Will My Child's Problem be Diagnosed?

Correct diagnosis is essential in the selection of the right treatment. Your professional needs to take the child's drug history. Very often there is multi-drug abuse, known as cross-addiction. Alcohol and marijuana is a popular combination. Parents are often surprised to learn the extent of their child's actual use; i.e. the frequency, the drugs involved or the combinations used. Parents, by the way, are not told of a child's drug history unless a release is signed by the child. At first, many children are angry that their parents have insisted on rehabilitation and refuse to sign. Anger is normal in the beginning. Be patient.

Should My Child be Drug Tested?

Ask your professional about the advisability of drug testing. Drug testing is a sensitive issue and parents often feel guilty asking their child to be tested. A drug screening, however, can be very effective when your adolescent keeps telling you that he is not using drugs and you instinctively know better. Some drugs, such as hallucinogens, do not show up in the urine. Urine testing needs to be carefully supervised because sometimes adolescents tamper with the specimen to achieve a negative result. Alcohol shows up in the urine for 12-24 hours, cocaine for 3-7 days, cannabis for 4-6 weeks, and barbiturates and amphetamines for about 4 weeks. It is important to get a urine sample as close to the time of suspected use as possible. If the child will cooperate, a blood test is more reliable.

What If My Child Won't Cooperate in Getting Treatment?

Professionals frequently recommend a *family intervention* to persuade an unwilling teen to accept treatment. Your professional will start by putting together a group made up of family members, appropriate close friends, and others (such as teachers or clergy) who are significant in the teen's life. Together, under the professional's guidance, the group will share information, evaluate the extent of the dependency and learn how the intervention ought to proceed.

A date and time are then set for a meeting with the child at which the group tries to collectively convince him/her to accept help. The intervention needs to be both *forceful* and *caring* to work. Sometimes the adolescent knows about the meeting and sometimes it is done by surprise. Professionals are trained in both formats.

At the intervention meeting, each group member presents evidence of the adolescent's irrational behavior as a result of his or her substance abuse. Each also expresses love and concern for the child who, it is hoped, will then be receptive to the idea of getting treatment.

In the course of the intervention, group members let the user know what the consequences are of continuing to drink/drug. For example parents might explain that they will no longer support him/her financially. They may stop paying college tuition. They make it clear that they will do nothing that will support his/her habit. Many therapists support the *Tough Love* concept which gives an adolescent the choice of quitting the substance abuse or leaving home. Talk to your professional before you take this approach.

An intervention may be appropriate when the abuse is first discovered. However, relapse can necessitate an intervention at any time during the recovery process.

Crisis interventions are sometimes necessary when drunken or stoned behavior gets out of control. Medical personnel, social workers or police who are trained in crisis intervention will go to the scene of trouble at any time of the day or night and intervene when behavior becomes violent or self-destructive in a life-threatening way. People who find themselves in such a situation should call nine-one-one (911) or their local hospital for help.

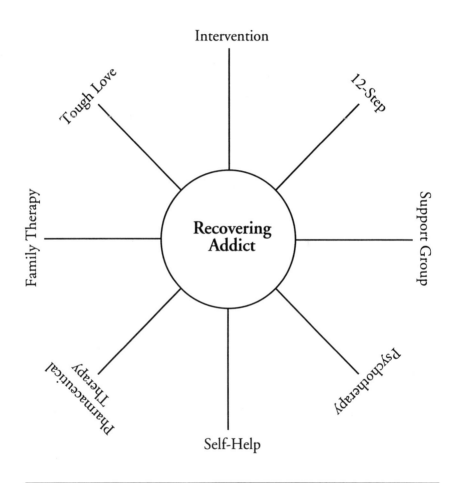

Intervention

Tough Love

12-Step

Family Therapy

Recovering
Addict

Support Group

Pharmaceutical
Therapy

Psychotherapy

Self-Help

Many routes can be taken to sobriety. There is no one correct answer as to how it should be accomplished.

Recovery

Once an adolescent has been diagnosed by a counselor or doctor as having a chemical addiction and the family has accepted the reality of the problem, the child is on the road to recovery. Many routes can be taken to sobriety and there is no single answer as to how it should be accomplished. The most important thing in getting help for a teenager or pre-teen is that you find a treatment professional who specializes in adolescent problems.

The key to recovery is to get the child to accept the fact that he is powerless over the substance and that its use will surely have disastrous consequences for him. Patience is essential. Family members are often frustrated by the fact that it's clear to them but not to the abuser how much damage the abuse is doing. The recovery effort is likely to fail if the child is not motivated.

Even when the first recovery effort succeeds, relapse is not uncommon with adolescents. If the addicted teen uses at all, he or she will abuse. Recovery will fail unless abstention is complete. Young people have a difficult time abstaining from alcohol or other drugs once they've formed the habit of using them. Peers encourage them to continue to abuse and society in general often condones underage drinking and illegal abuse of drugs. Parents buy kegs, advertisers plug alcohol and cigarettes, movies display drug use, rock stars glamorize it.

The addict experiences strong cravings roughly three months into the recovery period. It takes the better part of a year for these cravings to subside. Accordingly, ongoing family support is essential to the addict's recovery. The role of the family is discussed in detail in the Family Involvement section. But first, we will examine treatment options for the addict.

What Are the Treatment Options and Can I Afford Them?

A variety of treatment options are described in the pages which follow. Some are inpatient, and some are outpatient. Some provide ongoing aftercare. You need to discuss with your professional which options are appropriate and what they will cost. Costs vary greatly depending on whether your child needs outpatient or inpatient care; on whether the treatment is private or publicly funded; and on what the family of the patient is able to pay. Most therapists and treatment centers use a sliding pay scale. Don't let the issue of finances stand in the way of getting help.

Types of Therapy

There are four basic kinds of substance abuse therapy:

1. *Psychotherapy* — analysis conducted by psychologists, social workers, drug counselors and/or psychiatrists in order to understand the behavior underlying the alcohol or other drug abuse. Can be done on an inpatient or outpatient basis.

2. *Self-help* — support group help which is facilitated by non-professionals. The only qualification for admission is self-recognition of dependency and a desire to be helped. Usually outpatient.

3. *Family Therapy* — therapy facilitated by professionals in order to develop healthier interrelationships within the family. The goal is to resolve conflicts within the family and increase the support of family members for the adolescent. Can be inpatient or outpatient.

4. *Group Therapy* — professionals lead discussions of peers with the same problems as they share experiences and feelings. Can be inpatient or outpatient.

132

Inpatient Therapy

Inpatient residential facilities are sometimes available in a general hospital. But often they comprise a completely separate and independent medical facility. Their purpose is to purge the child's system of alcohol or other drugs, to get him or her to accept the fact that he/she has an addiction and to make him/her willing to modify future behavior to prevent future abuse.

When Is Inpatient Treatment Necessary?

- *When* your child's counselor recommends it. Get a second opinion if you wish, but don't fall into the denial trap of thinking "it's not really such a big problem".

- *When* your adolescent relapses and is not able to control his or her cravings despite counseling and AA. Dependence on alcohol or other drugs is a chronic relapsing disease. Parents must think of their recovering teen as being in remission — not cured.

- *When* monitored detoxification is necessary after prolonged, heavy binge drinking and/or extensive use of benzodiazapines, barbiturates, valium, opiates. People in this condition should be watched because heavy abusers can die from unmonitored detoxification.

- *When* your adolescent can no longer function in school.

- *When* your family's life as well as your teen's has become unmanageable because of his or her abuse of alcohol and other drugs.

- *When* the adolescent has no family and/or social support.

What Types of Inpatient Treatment Are Available?

Detoxification

An addict should never attempt to withdraw from his addiction without medical help. Withdrawal from alcohol or other drug addiction can cause seizures and convulsions. Inpatient detoxification takes roughly a week and is supervised by trained medical personnel. It allows a gradual and safe withdrawal, often accomplished by decreasing the dose of the drug on which the patient is dependent. Sometimes another drug is substituted in order to make withdrawal more comfortable.

Hospital

Today, many general care hospitals have in-house chemical dependence units, and some specialize in adolescent treatment. There are also treatment facilities which stand alone and specialize in addictions. The typical stay is 28 days, although this is not always possible where insurance is limited. During the stay, medical personnel work to free the addict of his addiction and therapists try to uncover the unresolved problems which have caused it. Costs range from free to very expensive. Fees should be discussed up front. Many hospitals will consider the patient's ability to pay.

Residential Therapeutic Communities (TC's)

Therapeutic communities came into existence in the 1950's. TC's identify the personal characteristics which led the addict to abuse drugs and then try to get the abuser to modify his or her behavior and develop a totally new life-style. Substance abusers in recovery live together within the TC and provide mutual reinforcement, companionship and positive peer pressure for the purpose of staying drug-free or sober. TC's are highly structured facilities. Their programs include encounter groups, education and residential jobs, such as cooking and cleaning. Length of stay ranges from 6 to 18 months. Frequently, staff have completed the recovery process and are therefore good role models. A high level of commitment is required and it is not unusual for patients to drop out.

Halfway Houses

A halfway house is a community-based, nonmedical facility which provides a transition from inpatient status to re-entry into society. People in recovery live in halfway houses where they are strictly supervised by psychologists and social workers. Some house only adolescents, while others mix ages. They are usually small, housing somewhere between 9 and 20 residents.

Typically, adolescents leave during the day to attend school or work. They return at day's end and participate in the life of the residence in an effort to prepare them for going home.

What Should I Look for in an Adolescent Treatment Center?

- *General Features* - Preferably, the adolescent unit should be separate from the adult unit. Senior staff members should have training in substance abuse and adolescent psychology. Initial evaluation should be thorough and last several hours. Steer away from a center which has a high turnover of staff.

- *Counseling* - Whether individual or group, counseling should be geared to self-help with the goal of having the addict take responsibility for himself and for his actions. Counselors should be certified. The ratio of patients to counselors should not exceed 8 to 1.

- *Family Involvement* - The facility should have a clearly stated plan for family involvement which spells out the scope and length of family participation. Family members may participate anywhere from 2 days to a full week. The center should be able to recommend family support groups in the area.

- *12-Step Programs* - The most successful addiction treatment over the years for both adults and adolescents has been that based on the 12-Step Program of Alcoholics Anonymous. The premise of the 12-Step Program is that the alcoholic must cure himself and that treatment professionals can only assist. Its power lies in its emphasis on spiritual rehabilitation and the fellowship that the process provides. (See 12-Step Programs, page 140.)

- *Physical Rehabilitation* - Because drugs and alcohol are so devastating to the adolescent body, rebuilding health through fitness and nutrition is a necessary function of a good treatment center.

- *After-care* - Look for a treatment center which promises to arrange for an after-care program when primary treatment ends. Good after-care eases the addict back into society after treatment and provides regular follow-up for as long as it is needed. Many teens relapse about three months after treatment; and sadly, some relapse again and again over a period of years. So, long-term after-care support can be vital in helping teens achieve long-term abstinence. To judge the effectiveness of an after-care program ask about the number and the activities of its alumni.

Outpatient Treatment

When Is Outpatient Treatment Appropriate?

If your teenager is motivated, accepts that he or she is powerless over the substance and is still able to function at school, then your professional may recommend outpatient treatment.

What Are the Outpatient Treatment Options?

Psychotherapy

Psychologists or social workers provide ongoing counseling to help adolescents see the negative consequences of alcohol or other drug abuse. Psychotherapy provides a safe and confidential forum for teens to vent their fears, anger and frustrations. The goal is to teach them how to cope with the stress in their lives and find healthier ways to deal with it. Styles of psychotherapy range from informal to highly structured.

Group Therapy

Group therapy gathers peers together who have the same concerns, feelings and self-realizations and can therefore support one another by sharing their experiences. Professionals lead group discussions. Group therapy can be powerful because people assimilate information quickly when it comes from peers who have suffered similar experiences or shared similar backgrounds. Peers can give each other understanding and empathy. In recent years, group therapy has extended to people with a variety of problems such as eating disorders, depression, divorce fallout or some other form of dysfunction.

Self-Help Groups

The self-help format is similar to the group therapy format. The difference is that peers help peers without the leadership of a professional. The 12-Step Alcoholics Anonymous and ALAnon Programs are examples of self-help groups.

Educational Model

By sharing information about the causes and effects of substance abuse, teachers attempt to get a youngster to see why he or she has chosen to abuse alcohol or other drugs and to consider wholesome alternatives. The educational model also teaches family members how to avoid the pitfalls of enabling continued abuse by the addict.

Emergency

For an outpatient emergency, call nine-one-one (911) or go to your local hospital emergency room. If you need crisis intervention (see page 129), give the location and describe the problem to the 911 dispatcher.

12-Step Programs

Because the 12-Step Program of Alcoholics Anonymous (AA) has helped so many people, both inpatient and outpatient therapists draw on it as a model to treat addicts. Even after therapy has stopped, many recovering addicts attend 12-Step Programs for years to reinforce their sobriety as part of their aftercare. The programs of Narcotics Anonymous (NA), Cocaine Anonymous (CA), ALAnon, NarAnon, ALAteen, and Overeaters Anonymous (OA), are based on AA's 12-Step Program.

The twelve spiritual guidelines of the Alcoholics Anonymous Program are called 'steps'. Members learn to live a sober life by following these steps, which are taught to them by other members who have been in the program for some time. Alcoholics learn these steps one at a time and it takes years for them to incorporate them into their lives. Alcoholics say that the program not only helps shake off the seductive appeal of drinking and/or drugging but also gives addicted young people and adults rules for living a more productive life.

The Program stresses that the recovering alcoholic must continually reinforce the 12-Step messages in order to stay sober. Addiction is a life-long problem. There is no cure, only treatment. Any use will draw the addict back into his addiction. The Program refers to alcoholics or drug addicts as recover*ing*, not recover*ed*.

Counselors suggest adolescents attend 12-Step Programs several times a week, especially in the beginning. Meetings usually take place in churches, hospitals or other meeting halls every day in urban and suburban areas. Rural towns have only one or two meetings a week.

To find a 12-Step meeting in your area, look in your local directory. Your treatment professional can tell you how to get connected to the Program which is right for your needs.

The 12 Steps

RECOVERY

Below are the Twelve Steps of Alcoholics Anonymous:

1. We admitted we were powerless over alcohol - that our lives had become unmanageable.

2. Came to believe that a Power greater than ourselves could restore us to sanity.

3. Made a decision to turn our will and our lives over to the care of God *as we understood Him.*

4. Made a searching and fearless moral inventory of ourselves.

5. Admitted to God, to ourselves and to another human being the exact nature of our wrongs.

6. Were entirely ready to have God remove all these defects of character.

7. Humbly asked Him to remove our shortcomings.

8. Made a list of all persons we had harmed, and became willing to make amends to them all.

9. Made direct amends to such people wherever possible, except when to do so would injure them or others.

10. Continued to take personal inventory and when we were wrong promptly admitted it.

11. Sought through prayer and meditation to improve our conscious contact with God, *as we understood Him,* praying only for knowledge of His will for us and the power to carry that out.

12. Having had a spiritual awakening as the result of these steps, we tried to carry this message to alcoholics, and to practice these principles in all our affairs.*

* See Alcoholics Anonymous World Services Inc. disclaimer on the *Cautions* page opposite the introduction to this book.

Aftercare

How Do I Keep My Child from Relapsing After Therapy?

An inpatient or outpatient program may motivate a child to cease abusing alcohol or other drugs and may reveal some of the unresolved problems leading to the child's substance abuse. But this is just the beginning. When an adolescent returns to the environment in which he or she was abusing alcohol or other drugs, there will be many temptations. Furthermore, the child may feel fragile, stressed or embarassed when faced with his peers. Staying sober will be a struggle and the teen will need ongoing aftercare for some time (perhaps years) to remain alcohol or drug free.

What Are the Aftercare Options?

12-Step Programs

12-Step Programs are a mainstay of every kind of treatment, including aftercare. The discussion on the previous pages underscores the need for an adolescent to continue with a 12-Step Program long after his treatment is completed.

School Support

In this country, public schools are mandated to provide drug awareness programs, and a few (but not very many) provide aftercare for recovering teens. If your public school does not offer such support, you and like-minded parents may want to encourage it to develop a recovery program. Such a program would include group meetings, as well as activities designed to immerse the teen in the life of the school.

Adolescent Re-Entry

Few communities have adequate programs to help youngsters re-enter school and social life. One such model re-entry program in Connecticut is called 'Project Rebound' which helps teens live alcohol and/or drug free and at the same time supports the family of the teen. Project Rebound forms a team which includes the recovering teen, his or her parents, a school counselor and a case manager. The case manager meets with the teenager weekly for up to ten months to monitor the child's progress and identify problems which could lead to relapse. He acts as an understanding and caring advocate, counseling the child and consults the school counselor to monitor progress. The child's parents are counseled in relapse prevention. Project Rebound also identifies resources which provide adolescents with a healthier lifestyle, such as sports, clubs, mentors and recreational activities. For information about Project Rebound, call (203) 363-2790.

Family Involvement

To this point this *Help For Parents* section has concerned itself with the addicted adolescent's role in recovery. The family also has a key part to play in helping the addicted child to stop his or her substance abuse. The next few pages will describe the process of family therapy, will address concerns that parents raise about the impact of the addict on family life, and will provide information about family support groups.

Why Does the Family of an Addict Need Therapy?

The family needs therapeutic help because each member in one way or another is continually tempted to adapt his or her actions to excuse, cover up or enable the addict's behavior. The family may end up being just as obsessed with the addict's drinking and drugging as the addict himself. In the grip of this obsession parents neglect children, family members drop friends, and responsibilities and outside interests fall by the way. Family members become frustrated because they can't control the addict's behavior and they turn on him in anger. Home becomes a battleground. Family members may be unaware that circumstances or behavior within the family have been contributing to the addict's substance abuse. For example, quarreling parents, lack of money, job loss or sickness often weigh on a youngster's mind more than anyone realizes.

Who Provides Family Therapy?

Your child's therapist will either provide family therapy or recommend a family specialist. Your treatment professional may also recommend an appropriate support group such as ALAnon.

Family Issues to Discuss with the Family Therapist?

This is a confusing time for the whole family. Many questions arise concerning the dynamics of a family in recovery. You may want to discuss the following issues with the family therapist.

Should We Consider a Family Intervention?

Often one of the first acts of the family is to participate in a family intervention to try to convince the addicted child to accept help. The intervention procedure is discussed in detail on pageS 128 and 129

How Do Family Members Enable an Addict to Continue His Abuse?

Family members often give in to the temptation to shoulder the addict's responsibilities and so preventing him from suffering the consequences of his irresponsible acts. Parents may lie for him at school, sometimes do his school work, and pay damages when he destroys the property of others. One parent may cover for the addict so that the other parent won't find out and get angry. Siblings may also cover for the addict or even take the blame for something the addict does so as to protect him.

Parents may mistakenly feel that they can <u>control</u> their child's recovery. The more they usurp the child's responsibilities, the less successful the recovery will be.

What If My Child Gets Violent, or Tries to Run Away?

Violence, suicide and running away are all possible side effects of substance abuse. Discuss with your therapist what to do if any of these crises should occur. Get an emergency contact so that you will be ready even if a crisis happens in the middle of the night. *Threats of suicide or running away should never be taken lightly.*

Now That My Child Is in Treatment, Will Our Family Life Return to Normal?

Parents often fall into the trap of thinking that after a few weeks of treatment, the problem will go away. This is just the beginning. Recovery is a life-long process for both the addict and his family. The family's continuing understanding and support for abstention are key to the young addict's recovery. Progress may be slow. Backsliding or relapse is common among adolescents. Don't get discouraged and don't ever give up on your child. Sometimes when the adolescent relapses the family relapses as well, falling back into denial and enabling behavior. You should be aware that it's easy for the whole family, as well as for the addict, to return to old habits.

Where Do I Find the Strength to Take Care of My Child for Such a Long Time?

Once your child is in good hands, you need to focus on yourself. Stay healthy - physically, mentally, emotionally. There are support groups designed to help you do this.

Where Do I Find Support for the Families of Addicts?

ALAnon and NarAnon are the two most prolific support groups, and they provide support for all members of the addict's family. ALAteen, which is less broadly established, is a program created by ALAnon to meet the special needs of siblings.

Basically, the support group teaches family members the three 'C's':

> "I didn't cause it."
> "I can't cure it."
> "I can't control it."

Once the addict is in treatment, the support program encourages family members to focus on themselves. They are taught how to avoid the co-dependent behavior which leads to strife within the family and which enables the addict to go on abusing alcohol or drugs. They are taught to stop spending their time worrying about the addict and trying to 'fix' his or her addiction. Rather, they learn ways to take care of themselves and each other and to turn their attention to other interests.

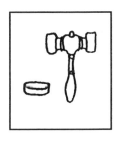

Legal Obligations

Do you know the penalties for violating the laws of your state relating to selling or serving alcohol, using or selling drugs and driving while intoxicated? It is important that both parents and teenagers understand their obligations under such laws and the legal penalties to which violations may expose them.

Serving Alcohol: Criminal Liability

Parents who serve alcohol to adolescents expose themselves to not one but two kinds of criminal liability. Simply *serving* alcohol to a minor (other than your own child) is illegal in many states; in Connecticut, for example, the penalty is a substantial fine or up to 18 months' imprisonment or both (Conn. General Statutes, Section 30-86).

In most states it is also a criminal offence to serve alcohol to someone who is *already intoxicated*. Although these state 'dram shop' laws were originally aimed at taverns, barrooms and the like, they have widened their scope to cover ordinary citizens serving drinks in private. Here is a typical provision:

> "Any person who sells, furnishes, gives or causes to be sold, furnished or given away, any alcoholic beverage to any habitual or common drunkard or to any obviously intoxicated person is guilty of a misdemeanor." (Criminal Liability — California Business and Professional Code, Section 25602). In California, a misdemeanor is punishable by imprisonment in the county jail for a period not exceeding six (6) months, or by a fine not exceeding $1,000 or by both. (California Penal Code, Section 19.)

The law may or may not be the same in your state; to understand it you will need to consult a local lawyer.

Serving Alcohol: Civil Liability

In California and some other states social hosts have no civil liability for damage or injury caused by an intoxicated minor (or adult) guest whom they have (over)served. But in other states the law does not shield parents from such liability. In 1988, for example, the Connecticut Supreme Court ruled in the case of *Ely vs. Murphy* that a social host could be found liable for negligently serving alcohol to a minor guest who injured another person while intoxicated. The court's decision overturned a long line of Connecticut cases which had shielded social hosts from such liability. In *Ely vs. Murphy* the defendant parent allegedly served alcohol at a graduation party to an 18 year-old boy who killed a 17 year-old guest with his car as he left the party. The 18 year-old driver subsequently committed suicide. The parents of the youth who was killed received $600,000 from the host in settlement of the lawsuit.

If the possible legal consequences do not deter you from serving alcohol to minors, consider the anguish of the families in this case.

Penalty for Possession of Marijuana

Penalties for marijuana possession vary from state to state. Generally speaking, laws which criminalize possession distinguish between small amounts meant for personal use and larger amounts associated with cultivation, delivery and sale. All states impose fines for *any* possession and some go further by imposing jail sentences or community service requirements for possession of even small amounts.

Personal-use fines vary widely, from as little as $100 to as much as $150,000. Personal-use jail sentences also range widely, from 0-15 years. Community service requirements go as high as 100 hours.

Penalties for cultivation, delivery and sale (trafficking) tend to be more severe, with fines in some states reaching $1,000,000. Jail sentences range from 0 to life. For this purpose some states impose the same penalties for marijuana dealing as those for hard drug trafficking. Consult a local lawyer to learn what penalties your state imposes.

Drunk Driving Laws

Whether someone can be convicted of drunk driving depends on his or her blood alcohol content (BAC) at the time of arrest. Almost all states allow a driver to be convicted merely upon proof that his or her BAC exceeded the legal minimum, which in most states is 0.10. Several states, however, have recently lowered the BAC requirement to 0.08. Some states have set a special *zero tolerance* BAC level for underaged drinkers. Zero tolerance laws allow police to impose penalties on drivers under 21 *if any* alcohol is found in their blood at the time of arrest.

In the next paragraph, the authors describe the drunk driving arrest process in their home state of Connecticut. The process is similar in most other states, and *insurance costs go up in every state following a conviction for drunk driving.* State police in your area can tell you how your state's penalties vary from those in Connecticut.

Connecticut's Drunk Driving Laws (3)

If arrested for driving while intoxicated:

- You will be detained by the police and read your rights.

- Your car will be towed at your expense.

- You will be taken in a police cruiser to the police station.

- You will be asked to submit to a blood alcohol content (BAC) test. If you refuse, your license will be administratively suspended for six months and the cost of your auto insurance will go up.

- If you take the test and it registers a BAC of more than .07 but below .10, you will be held with a presumption that you were driving while impaired.

- If the test registers .10 or over, you will be held with a presumption that you were driving while intoxicated.

- You will be kept in a lock-up until you are bailed out.

If your BAC reads .10 or above, administrative penalties dictate that:

- Your license will be automatically revoked for 24 hours by the police. You will thereafter be issued a temporary license. This temporary license will be suspended by the DMV no later than 35 days after your arrest, pending a limited hearing to which you are entitled during this period.

- Your license will be suspended for 90 days at .10 or for six months if you refuse to take a BAC test.

- Your license will be suspended for one year for a second offense and for two years for every offense thereafter.

If your BAC reads .10 or above and you are convicted under criminal law:

- You will be fined $500 to $1,000 for the first offense, up to $2,000 for the second, up to $4,000 for the third and up to $8,000 for the fourth.

- You will serve a mandatory two-day jail sentence, and the judge may sentence you up to six months or to 100 hours of community service for the first offense. For the second offense, you will serve 10 days to one year in jail and for the third, 20 days to two years.

- Your license will be suspended for one year or until you reach age 18, whichever is longer, for the first offense. For the second offense, it will be suspended for two years; for the third, three years; and for the fourth, it will be permanently revoked.

A Word about BACs

Some commentators warn that even the .10 or .08 BAC requirements are too high because they can allow some people to drive legally after having as many as *three or four drinks.* They point out that the intoxicating effect of alcohol can be increased by a number of factors — an empty stomach, menstruation, lack of tolerance and medications. A driver with low tolerance or an empty stomach, for example, can suffer dulled reflexes and lack of coordination after only *one drink.* A driver taking a particular medication can pass out or become ill after one drink. Even if the legal BAC level in your state tolerates considerable drinking, it's always best to follow a policy of *not drinking and driving.*

The Price You'll Pay for Driving Drunk

Towing your car.	.$ 50
Car storage for one day	15
Defense attorney.	1,000
Minimum fine.	500
Increased insurance rate.	3,976*
Total.	$ 5,541

Add to this total a possible $500 for Alcohol Education Program fee.

Your insurance company will probably drop you and you will become an assigned risk. Certain companies will insure assigned risk cases for a greatly increased fee. The figure quoted is an average fee for someone who is designated an assigned risk.

National Toll-free Hotlines and Helplines

If you are seeking information or treatment, one of the national toll-free telephone numbers listed below may help.

Drugs and Alcohol

National Cocaine Hotline 800-COCAINE
24-hour, 7 day/wk service; information and referral.

National Alcohol Hotline 800-ALCOHOL
24-hour, 7 day/wk service; information and referral.

National Institute for Drug Referral Helpline . 800-662-HELP
9 a.m. - 3:00 a.m., Mon. thru Fri. (E.S.T.);

12 noon - 3:00 a.m., Sat. and Sun. (E.S.T.); information, referral and support.

Eating Disorders

Gracie Sq. Eating Disorders Helpline 800-382-2832
24-hour, 7 day/wk service; information on bulimia and/or anorexia, referral.

Runaways

Runaway Hotline 800-231-6946
24-hour 7 day/wk counseling, referral to emergency shelter, transportation, medical and legal help for parents and children aged 5 to 18. Confidential relay of messages to parents without revealing locations.

National Runaway Switchboard 800-621-4000
24-hour 7 day/wk counseling and referral sevices for runaways and their parents.

154

Educational Materials on Substance Abuse

Drug Watch International .... **(915) 837-3500**
.... **or FAX: (915) 364-0023**

P.O. Box 1022
Alpine, TX 79831

Drug Watch International is an advocacy organization which promotes the creation of healthy, drug free cultures worldwide and opposes the legalization and decriminalization of drugs. Its members are volunteers who provide an international communications network and referral system.

Elks Drug Awareness Program .... **FAX: (205) 825-4422**

Route 1, Box 62
Jackson's Gap, Alabama 36861

Drug-related free pamphlets can be obtained from the headquarters listed above or from your local Elks lodge.

**National Clearinghouse for Alcohol
and Drug Information** **800-729-6686**

Prevention materials and information including brochures, posters, videotapes, resource guides, directories, program descriptions and drug surveys.

National Families in Action .... **FAX: (404) 934-7137**

2296 Henderson Mill Road, Suite 204
Atlanta, GA 30345

Tapes and printed information on alcohol and other drug related subjects, including an excellent periodical publication called Drug Abuse Update.

Hazelden **800-328-9000**

Educational materials on alcohol, drugs, nicotine, gambling and all addictions.

AIDS

AIDS Hotline **800-342-AIDS**

24-hour, 7 day/wk Public Health Service information on AIDS.

Support Groups:

Headquarters are listed, '800' numbers not available. Many towns will have local chapters which will be listed in your telephone directory.

Alcoholics Anonymous (AA) .... **(212) 870-3400**
General Service Office Board
P.O. Box 459
Grand Central Station
New York, NY 10163

Treatment and support for people addicted to alcohol. Most areas have programs for adolescents and young adults. Contact your local chapter and inquire about such programs.

ALANON and ALATEEN .... **(212) 302-7240**
P.O. Box 862
Madison Square Station
New York, NY 10018

Treatment and support for people living with an addict or alcoholic.

Cocaine Anonymous (CA) .... **(310) 559-5833**
3740 Overland Avenue, Suite H
Los Angeles, CA 90034

Treatment and support for people addicted to cocaine.

Narcotics Anonymous (NA) .... **(818) 780-3951**
World Service office
P.O. Box 9999
Van Nuys, CA 91409

Treatment and support for people addicted to narcotics.

NAR-ANON Family Group headquarters .... **(310) 547-5800**
World Service Office
P.O. Box 2562
Palos Verdes Peninsula, CA 902774

Support for people living with an addict.

Toughlove .... **(215) 348-7090**
P.O. Box 1069
Doylestown, PA 18901

Support for parents of children with behavioral problems.

Statistical References

Prevention:

Effective Parenting, page 8.
    1. Parent's Music Resource Center, Arlington, VA. 2. NIAAA, *7th Report to Congress.*

Parents and Community, page 11
    1. Office of Substance Abuse Prevention (OSAP), Monograph 6, *Youth and Drugs: Society's Mixed Messages.*

Party Guidelines, page 25.
    1. National Highway Traffic Safety Administration (N.H.T.S.A.), 1990.

Problems:

Statistics, pages 33 and 34.
    1. National Household Survey on Drug Abuse, 1990, by the National Institute on Drug Abuse (NIDA). 2. American Anorexia Bulimia Association. 3. The Alan Guttmacher Institute, Washington, D.C., *"Facts in Brief",* 1991. 4. National Institute of Alcohol Abuse and Alcoholism (NIAAA), *Alcohol and Health* monograph. 5. Reprinted from *The PRIDE Questionnaire Report, 1991/92 National Summary for Grades 6 to 12,* with permission of PRIDE (The Parents Resource Institute for Drug Education), Atlanta, GA. 6. OSAP, Prevention Pipeline, May/June 1991. 7. OSAP, Prevention Pipeline, March/April 1989. 8. American Cancer Society, Atlanta, GA. 9. Cocaine Hotline Survey (800-COCAINE). 10. Journal of the American Medical Association, Chicago, IL. 11. United Way, *It's Never Too Early to Talk to Your Young Children About Drugs.* 12. *Drug Use Among American High School Seniors, College Students and Young Adults, 1975–1990,* University of Michigan Institute for Social Research, L.D. Johnston et al.

Alcohol and Drug Use Among School Children, pages 35 and 36.
    1. High Five America, San Diego, CA. 2. United Way, *It's Never Too Early...,* as above. 3. Gallup Poll. 4. *Promoting Adolescent Health,* N.P. Gordon and A. McAllister, Adolescent Drinking: Issues and Research, Academia Press, New York, 1982. 5. Center for Science in the Public Interest, Wash., D.C. 6. OSAP, Prevention Pipeline, May/June 1991. 7. NIDA. 8. *Drug Use, Drinking and Smoking,* L.D. Johnson et. al. 9. *PRIDE Questionnaire, 1993/1994,* as above. OSAP, Prevention Pipeline, May/June 1991. 10. U. of Michigan Survey, 1992, L. D. Johnston et al.

Suicide, Crime, Sex and Eating Disorders, page 37.
    1. National Center for Health Statistics, Maryland. 2. *Family Circle,* New York, NY. 3. Centers for Disease Control, Atlanta, GA., 1990 surveys. 4.*Drug Use Among American High School Seniors, College Students and Young Adults, 1975–1990,* University of Michigan Institute for Social Research, L.D. Johnston et al. 5. Anti-Drug Abuse Act of 1988.

157

Trends and Insights, pages 38 and 39.
1. *The New York Times,* October 1, 1991. 2. *PRIDE Questionnaire, 1991/92* as above. 3. Alan Guttmacher Institute, Washington, D.C. 4. NIDA 5. JAMA, Vol. 268, No. 12, 1992.

Sobering Statistics, pages 40 and 41.
1. National Council on Alcoholism and Drug Dependence (NCADD), Washington, D.C. 2. N.H.T.S.A., 1990. 3. *Insurance Institute for Highway Safety Fatality Facts, 1990,* Arlington, VA. 4. Fatality Facts 1992 Insurance Institute for Highway Safety. 5. NIAAA, *Alcohol Health & Research Vol.9, #4* 6. National Transportation Safety Board. 7. M. Bernstein, J. Mahoney. *Occupational Medicine, Vol. 4, #2* 8. NIAAA, *7th Report to Congress, Alcohol & Health.*

Why Drugs and Alcohol? pages 43 to 45.
1. NIAAA, *7th Special Report to Congress.* 2. Parent's Music Resource Center, Arlington, VA.

The Media, Television Violence, pages 53-55.
1. *News from Paul Simon on Senate Hearings,* Tuesday, June 8, 1993. 2. *Violence and Youth: Psychology's Response,* American Psychological Association, Washington, DC, 1993. 3. *Connections,* Prothow, Stith, D., Harvard U. School of Public Health, Cambridge, MA, Winter 1992/93.

The Media, Advertising, pages 56-57.
1. *The New York Times,* February 17, 1993. 2. *Myths, Men & Beer: An Analysis of Beer Commercials on Broadcast Television,* AAA Foundation for Traffic Safety, Washington, DC, 1987. 3. *Reports on Youth and Alcohol,* Office of Inspector General, Dept. of Health and Human Services, 1991. 4. AAA Foundation for Traffic Safety, Washington, DC. 5. *Citizens' Action Handbook on Alcohol and Tobacco Billboard Advertising,* Center for Science in the Public Interest, Washinton, DC.

First Amendment, pages 58-61.
1. Hentoff, *Free Speech for Me—But Not for Thee,* HarperCollins, 1992, p. 369. 2. *The New York Times,* July 1, 1995, p. A7, *Action for Children's Television v. FCC,* decided June 30, 1995.

Alcohol, page 64.
1. NIDA Notes, Spring 1991. 2. Harvard University Study of Mass. College Students, 1989. 3. RID National Newsletter, Fall 1993, Schenectedy, NY. 4. NIAAA, *Alcohol, Tobacco and Other Drugs May Harm the Unborn,* Cook, Peterson and Moore. 5. U.S. Dept. of Health & Human Services, Rockville, MD.

Cigarettes, page 68.
1. *The CATOR Report, one year outcome results for adolescents,* St. Paul, MN, 1991.

Smokeless Tobacco, page 69.
  1. *National Household Survey on Drug Abuse, 1990,* NIDA.

Marijuana, page 70.
  1. Potency Monitoring Project 1992, University of Mississippi. 2. Medical College of Virginia, Dr. Guy Cabral.

Cocaine, page 76.
  1. *NIDA Notes,* Spring 1991, NIDA. 2. *Cocaine SPECT Scanning,* Sabah Tumeh, M.D., Ph.D. at Harvard University, Boston, MA.

Amphetamines, page 78.
  1. *Uppers, Downers and All Arounders,* Anaba and Cohen, Cinemed, Inc., Ashland, OR; 1989.

Steroids, page 82.
  1. *Sports Illustrated,* July 8, 1991 2. *Drug Abuse Update*, National Families in Action, Atlanta, GA. 3. Radar Target Resource Center, Kansas City, MO.

HGH, page 85.
  1. JAMA, Vol. 269, No. 11, 1993.

Inhalants, page 86.
  1. *Mood Altering Chemical Series: Inhalants,* Wisconsin Clearinghouse, Madison, WI.

LSD, pages 89 and 90.
  1. The Chemical People, Winter 1992/3. 2.   NIDA.
Valium, page 97.
  1. *Uppers, Downers,* etc., as above.

Multi Drug Use, page 99.
  1. *Teen Drug Use,* Bishner and Friedman, Lexington Books, Lexington, MA. 2. *Cocaine Hotline Survey* (800-COCAINE). 3. *NIDA Notes, Spring 1991,* NIDA. 4. *Uppers, Downers,* as above.

Teenage Sexual Activity, page 114.
  1. Alan Guttmacher Institute, Washington, D.C., *Facts in Brief,* 1994. 2. Centers for Disease Control, Atlanta, GA. 3. *Journal of Marriage and the Family.*

Suicidal Feelings, page 115.
  1. National Center for Health Statistics.

Drug Dealing and Crime, page 117 to 119.
  1. *Survey of Youth in Custody,* Department of Justice, Office of Justice Programs, Washington, D.C., 1987 2. F.B.I., *Uniform Crime Reports, Crime in the U.S.,* 1990 3. White House Conference for a Drug Free America, Final Report. 4. *Research in Brief,* National Institute of Justice, U.S. Department of Justice, Washington, D.C., 1990.

Recommended Books

The books listed below are recommended reading for all parents of adolescents. Your local library or bookstore should be able to obtain any one of them for you.

Books

- *Don't Stop Loving Me: A Reassuring Guide for Mothers of Adolescent Daughters*, Ann F. Caron, Ed.D., Henry Holt, January 1991.

  "Adolescents withhold information about the local party scene because they want to shield (rather than shock) their parents. Parents can help their students by calmly acknowledging the local situation, admitting its allure, and helping their children think of ways to withstand the social pressures."

- *Strong Mothers, Strong Sons, Raising Adolescent Boys in the 90's,* Ann F. Caron, Ed.D., Henry Holt, 1994.

  "Mothers who presume that their sons will turn out fine seem to have sons who fulfull those expectations. But beliefs need reinforcement through action."

- *Parenting Isn't For Cowards,* James Dobson, World Books, 1987.

  "His parents watch apprehensively as he climbs aboard a capsule called adolescence and waits for his rockets to fire. His father and mother wish they could go with him, but there is room for just one person in the spacecraft. Besides, nobody invited them."

- *All Grown Up and No Place To Go,* David Elkind, Addison-Wesley Publishing Co., 1984.

  "High schools which were once the setting for a unique teenage culture have become miniatures of the adult community."

- *How to Talk So Your Kids Will Listen, How to Listen So Your Kids Will Talk,* Faber, Avon Books, New York.

  "The way parents see their children can influence not only the way children see themselves, but also the way they behave."

- *Uppers, Downers, All Arounders,* Darryl Inaba, Pharm.D. and William Cohen, Cinemed, Inc. Ashland, OR, 1989.

  "As long as we, the highest order of life on Earth, have had to think, we've searched for ways to alter our state of consciousness. Whether we've wanted to forget our harsh surroundings, come to grips with our mortality, alter our mood, explore feelings, promote social interaction or enhance our senses, we've felt a desire to tinker with reality."

- *Why Johnny Can't Tell Right From Wrong,* William K. Kilpatrick, Simon and Schuster, 1992.

  "Teaching right from wrong has as much bearing on a culture's survival as teaching reading, writing or science, and there exists a great wealth of knowledge about how to do it."

- *The Road Less Traveled,* M. Scott Peck, M.D., Simon and Schuster, New York.

  "Life is difficult. This is a great truth...It is a great truth because once we truly see this truth, we transcend it."

About the Authors

Leigh Rudd

"I just wasn't prepared when my 16-year-old son said to me, "Mom, I'm a drug addict." "How could it be?" I thought. This was a responsible, outgoing, popular kid, a 3-letter athlete, an attractive young man — a kid everyone wanted to know.

"My life suddenly changed. I found myself immersed in a nightmare of turmoil, fear and painful questions I couldn't answer. Why had this happened? It was 1986, a time when adolescent substance abuse was a carefully kept secret. Getting information at that time was very difficult. There was a stigma; 'nice' families didn't have drug problems. Denial reigned. Parents did not share their concerns about their teens drinking and drugging; it was frequently kept secret because reputations were at stake.

"As soon as my son shared this crisis with me, I started networking frantically around the clock to find other parents who had this problem. I needed information. I was desperate. I feared for his life much of the time. There were many lonely and frightening moments as my attempts to find help were frustrated. It took months of trial and error before we were firmly entrenched in a recovery program. Because there was so little information available, we made many mistakes.

"I can now say, several years later, that my son is doing extremely well. It was because of this personal experience that I was inspired to write *The Parents' Pipeline Guide,* sharing my insights and information. Perhaps I can help another mother or father recognize the signs of substance abuse earlier than I did and avert a tragedy."

Leigh Rudd, the mother of three, lives in Greenwich, CT with her husband. Ms. Rudd spent 20 years in the fashion industry as the founder and president of an international publishing company. As a result of her own child's substance abuse problem she volunteered to co-author *The Greenwich Parents' Prevention Handbook,* which was the forerunner of *The No-Nonsense Parents' Guide* and *The Parents' Pipeline Guide.* Ms. Rudd has testified in Washington for Senator Christopher Dodd on adolescent substance abuse, produced radio shows on the subject and appeared on TV.

Sheila Fuller

Sheila Fuller lives in Greenwich, CT with her husband and two
adolescent children. She is the past President of
The Greenwich Council on Youth and Drugs
and co-author of *The Greenwich Parents' Prevention Handbook*, a forerunner of *The No-Nonsense Parents' Guide* and *The Parents' Pipeline Guide*,
which was mailed to parents of adolescents
throughout the Greenwich community. Parents
who received it felt that such a book filled a need

because they were distressed about teenage behavior, but didn't know
what to do about it. Mrs. Fuller believes that *The Parents' Pipeline Guide*,
which is written for a larger audience, will be just as useful.

Mrs. Fuller also serves on the United Way of Greenwich Suicide
Prevention Task Force and is a member of the Lower Fairfield County
Action Against Chemical Dependency, a council set up to develop and
coordinate Connecticut Alcohol and Drug Abuse Commission (CADAC)
services in lower Fairfield County.

Mrs. Fuller worries that in today's world far too many young people
are not making the journey through adolescence successfully. Epidemic
numbers emerge from their teens addicted to alcohol and drugs. Others
are traumatized by premature sexual relationships and experiences, and
many more are jaded from trying to cope with the problems of the adult
world long before becoming equipped to handle them. Through her
work, she is committed to raising parent awareness of teen substance use
and related problems so that more parents will join the growing ranks of
adults who are making a difference in young people's lives.